THE SCIENCE OF RELIGION

OR

SANATANA VAIDIKA DHARMA

THE SCIENCE OF RELIGION

OR

SANATANA VAIDIKA DHARMA

AN ATTEMPT AT AN EXPOSITION OF PRINCIPLES

BY

BHAGAVAN DAS

GYAN

Published by

GYAN

Gyan Publishing House
5, Ansari Road
Daryaganj, New Delhi-110002
Phone: 011-47034999, 9811692060
E-mail: books@gyanbooks.com

Distribution Network
gyanbooks.com
India, USA, Canada, UK, Australia

ISBN: 978-93-6208-183-4 (HB)
First Published, 1917

2nd Impression 2024

Printed at: Gyan Press, Delhi.

THE SCIENCE OF RELIGION OR SANATANA VAIDIKA DHARMA
Author: BHAGAVAN DAS

ॐ

THE SCIENCE OF RELIGION

OR

SANATANA VAIDIKA DHARMA

AN ATTEMPT AT AN EXPOSITION OF
PRINCIPLES

BY

BHAGAVAN DAS.

'UBLISHED BY BABU AMBIKA KANTA CHAKRAVARTI,

KAMACHHA, BENARES.

FOREWORD.

For that same reason for which the Oversoul of the Human Race has brought together the modern West and the ancient East, is it desirable to clothe for the time being the ancient mind in the garb of a modern language. Some disapprove of 'modernism' in religion, but others say that it is Nature's own way to preserve the continuity of the essential Spirit by perpetually redressing it in the fresh garments of infant morn from the decayed vestures of aged yestereven.

Living organisms, it is said, lose vital reproductive power and freshness after a series of fissiparous or endogamous generations; but recover it by conjugation or cross-fertilisation. Even so do the thoughts, the ideals, the ways, of human communities require exogamous alliances with new forms of expression for a new lease of richer life. And honest exchange of commodities, spiritual as well as material, is profitable to both the parties concerned. Hence these efforts—unfortunately too feeble, because of the incompetence of the instrument—to reinterpret old ideas in new terms.

Readers who may happen to become interested in the lines of thought suggested here, will find fuller details and other aspects and developments of the three main parts of this work, dealing respectively with Knowledge, Feeling, and Action, in the writer's other compilations, *viz.*, *The Science of Peace*, *The Science of the Emotions*, and *The Science of Social Organisation* (or *The Laws of Manu*) respectively, and a summation and general survey in *The Science of the Sacred Word* (or *The Pranava-Vāḍa of Gārgyāyaṇa*) Various other pamphlets of his also endeavour to illustrate and apply to current problems the same root-principles and ideas of Sanāṭana Vaiḍika Ḍharma—the Universal Religion which lays down the foundations for a Universal Society, an organisation of the whole Human Race, on the lines of Universal Science. For such is its distinctive feature. While the founders of most other religions concern themselves mainly with the individual and seek to purify and elevate him along some one particular line, leaving it to him to arrange the affairs of his community as he thinks best, this, the all-comprehensive, all-synthesising Ḍharma (not identified with any one name) deals not only with the individual, in all his main types and stages of evolution in this and the other worlds, but also lays down the foundations for the domestics, the economics and the politics of mankind; in short, provides a complete scheme of life, individual as well as communal.

Note:—To his great regret, the writer finds that he is not able to bring out this work in the complete form he had projected. Chapters of it have appeared in the *Central Hindū College Magazine*, at intervals, during the years 1914 and 1915. There has been a break now for a year and a half, owing to illnesses and to distractions caused by unavoidable other work. Not knowing whether, and when if at all, he would be able to complete the work as planned, he has thought it best to place before the public in book-form the portion that has been done.

At the end of the table of contents will be found an outline of the remaining portion of the project.

Benares, 21st March, 1917.

CONTENTS.

CHAPTER I.

CHAPTER II.

CHAPTER III.

CHAPTER IV.

Note:—The rest of the work should deal with the remaining two heads of Niṭya-karma, viz. (*c*) Agni-kārya, the tending of the various Fires, physical and superphysical, (*d*) Sanḍhyā-vanḍanam or Worship and Prayer. Then should come Naimiṭṭika-karma with its main subdivisions: (*a*) The pre-natal and natal sacraments and pre-cautionary and helpful observances, or Eugenics; (*b*) Upanayana or Education. spiritual, mental and physical; (*c*) Vivāha or Marriage; (*d*) Maraṇa-samskāra or funeral and post mortem sacraments and ceremonies for the helping of the departed soul in other worlds. Thereafter should follow a section on Kāmya-karma, dealing with various "sacrifices," or special enterprises undertaken for special ends. Finally, there should be a chapter on the culture-civilisation founded on and developed by Sanāṭana Vaiḍika Ḍharma, in the past, in India, and expressing itself in (*a*) the intellectual, or scientific and philosophic, (*b* the emotional, or artistic and domestic, and (*c*) the actional, or domestic, political and economical life of the Indian people, with reference to Varṇa and Āshrama, *i. e.*, types or classes of men and stages of life.

VAIDIKA DHARMA

A Brief Study in 'Religions and Religion'.

I. The Nature and Constituents of Vaidika Dharma.

(*i*) *Ideals.*

SCIENTIFIC Religion—a religion of science—a science of religion—a science and a religion in mutual friendship and support and co-operation, bound together in indissoluble bonds of logic and consistency, a reconciliation of head and heart, a holy and happy marriage of strong Reason and beauteous Emotion with multifarious progeny of noble Actions, —such is the despair of the present, and at most a tantalising dream of the future, for the modern 'civilised' mind.

Enormous labor has been expended by that mind on the study of 'religion', of 'comparative religion,' and now, in the last few years, on 'the psychology of religion'—a 'science' of very recent birth. This is the natural order of progress in all departments of knowledge, first observation, then comparison, then examination and investigation into root-causes. As said in the *Nyāya-Bhāshya* (I, i, 2.)

त्रिविधा चास्य शास्त्रस्य प्रवृत्तिः, उद्देशः, लक्षणं, परीक्षा चेति ।

And in the study of the *psychology* of religion is the hope of 'the dream of the future' being realised by that modern civilised mind. Truly admirable is the industry of that young, vigorous, enterprising, self-dependent mind along all the lines of knowledge. It despises the old! It will not take what is given to it ready-made! It must achieve and conquer for itself! May it conquer the kingdom of heaven, may it achieve the Truth of Religion, the Spirit of Righteousness very early—along these lines of *psychology*—lest and before the unchecked forces of over-energetic egoistic turbulence prevail and become able to hurl the nations into devastating wars and fling humanity back into the long darknesses of the barbarous ages!

A writer in the *Hibbert Journal*, not very long ago, discussing the causes which were enfeebling, endangering and bringing decadence upon civilisation in the west—which enfeeblement and decadence he affirmed positively—went on to say, "The remedies lie in the modern man's......more exact knowledge of *the laws of evolution and psychology*". Prof. Bergson, whose philosophy is very much in vogue at present in Europe, in his address, delivered as President of the Psychical Research Society, in May 1913, spoke "regarding the developments that would have followed if all our science for the last three centuries had been devoted to the study of the mind rather than of matter. If Kepler, Galileo, and Newton had been psychologists, the study of mind would have attained heights comparable only to the level on which astronomy and physics now stand. Biology would have advanced on vitalist lines; we should have had a therapeutics based on 'suggestion'; *psychical research*, instead of needing a society to advance it, would hold the place that physics now occupies, and, instead, we might have had a society for *physical* research." He went on to say, "But it was not desirable that things should have thus developed. There would have been wanting that scientific precision, the anxiety for proof, the habit of distinguishing that which is certain from that which is simply possible or probable. With the precision, the rigour, and the scruples which the physical sciences have produced in the investigator, and renouncing the bad metaphysics which embarrassed research, *the science of mind* would attain results surpassing all our hopes." The Hinḍū reader who remembers the *Yoga-Ḍarshana* here, and remembers that it is veritably Practical or Applied Psychology, the Art of Psychology—whereby different states of consciousness, *Jāgrat*, *Svapna*, *Sushupti*, etc., —now working on comparatively disconnected planes, in comparatively disconnected worlds, the waking-world, the dream-world, the slumber-world, or *Bhūh*, *Bhuvah*, *Svah*, etc., can be linked up, and many physical and superphysical powers now latent in man can be developed—such reader will realise the full practical bearing of Prof. Bergson's remarks; their practical bearing on the methods of education and research, in West and East, which naturally supplement each other and make up a perfect whole. What the East has dropped and lost in the hurried and stormy march of time, of her possessions in the department of *physical* research, it may regain by its contact with the West. What the West has not yet found in the department of *psychical* research, it may find at least clues to, and hints of, through its 'conquest' of the East, and develop and promulgate anew and more quickly for the benefit of the world. Happy indeed would the time be when physics and psychics, religion and science, meet and combine for the common good.

(ii) *Western views of Religion.*

In the meanwhile, what have western scholars to say as to the nature and uses,. if any, of Religion? The latest and most authoritative Dictionary of the English Language—the *Cen-*

tury—gives such definitions: "(1) Recognition of and allegiance in manner of life to some superhuman power or powers, to whom allegiance and service are regarded as justly due. (2) The healthful development and right life of the spiritual nature, as contrasted with that of the mere intellectual and social powers. (3) Any system of faith in and worship of a divine Being or beings. (4) The rites or services of religion; the practice of sacred rites and ceremonies." And the work quotes others of the more famous definitions. Thus, J. Martineau: "By religion I understand the belief and worship of Supreme Mind and Will, directing the universe and holding moral relations with human life." And J. H. Newman: "By Religion I mean the knowledge of God, of his will, and of our duties towards him." And Matthew Arnold: "Religion.........is ethics heightened, enkindled, lit up by feeling;" morality *plus* emotion. Latimer: "Pure Religion.........standeth.........in righteousness, justice and well doing." "Religion is the communion between a worshipping subject and a worshipped object—the communion of a man with what he believes to be a God." (*Faiths of the World*).

The latest edition of the *Encyclopædia Britannica*—handbook of omniscience up to date—gives prominence to two definitions; Tylor's: "Religion is the belief in spiritual beings"; and Frazer's: "Religion is a propitiation or conciliation of powers superior to man which are believed to direct and control the course of nature and of human life". And the writer of the article after duly pointing out the defects of these, puts forward his own suggestion that the missing and much-hunted secret is to be found in a due dissection of the notion of "the Sacred", which he believes to run through all forms and views of religion. And he accordingly discusses that notion threadbare. "The Sacred" as (1) the forbidden, (2) the mysterious, (3) the secret, (4) the potent, (5) the animate, and (6) the ancient; then, the activity of "the Sacred" in its aspects of (1) fecundity, (2) ambiguity, (3) relativity, and (4) transmissibility; and finally, "the methods of the exploitation of the Sacred", viz., by (1) acquisition, (2) concentration, (3) induction, (4) renovation, (5) insulation, and (6) direction—such are the sub-titles of his theme and the objects of his industrious labor—all most *informing* undoubtedly, but not *satisfying* to either head or heart.

The following extracts are taken from a useful little book by Leuba on *The Psychological Origin and the Nature of Religion.* "The students of Religion have usually been content to describe it, either in *intellectual* or in *affective* terms. 'This particular idea or belief' or 'this particular feeling or emotion' is, they have said, 'the essence' or the 'vital element' of Religion. So that most of the hundreds of definitions which have been proposed fall into two classes. We have, on the one hand, the definitions of Spencer, Max Muller, Romanes, Goblet d'Alviella, and others, for whom Religion is 'the recognition of a mystery pressing for investigation' or 'a department of thought', or 'a belief in superhuman beings'; and, on the other, the formulas of Schleiermacher, the Ritschlian theologians, Tiele, etc., who hold that Religion is 'a 'feeling of absolute dependence upon God', or 'that pure and reverential disposition or frame of mind we call piety.' According to Tiele 'the essence of piety, and therefore of Religion, is adoration.' As these amazing discrepancies and contradictions ....arise primarily from a faulty *psychology*, a moment may profitably be devoted to an untechnical statement of the present teaching of that science upon the relation existing between *the three acknowledged modes of Consciousness, willing, feeling and thinking*...Every pulse of consciousness is practically compounded of will, feeling and thought. ...To-day it has (therefore) become customary to admit that 'in Religion all sides of the personality participate. Will, feeling and intelligence are necessary and inseparable constituents of Religion.' Religion .....is compounded of will, thought and feeling, bearing to each other the relation which belongs to them in every department of life. And it will, moreover, be clear that a purpose or an ideal, i.e., something to be attained or maintained, must always be at the root of it. ......Religion, then is a particular kind of *activity*, a mode or *type of behavior*......impossible to identify with a particular emotion, or a particular belief." Then Leuba goes on to describe, in successive chapters, the three main types of behavior (1) mechanical, (2) coercitive or magical, and (3) anthropopathic, or Religious; the origin of the ideas of ghosts, nature-beings and gods, out of (*a*) swoons, trances, etc., (*b*) hallucinations, (*c*) spontaneous personifications, (*d*) the search for causes; the distinction between and the mutual relations of Religion, Magic and Science; primitive religious emotion; and finally, the nature and the function of religion, —all very elaborate, and, as in the other cases, full of straining to achieve minute analytical distinctions (on the Nyāya maxim,

अणुरपि विशेषोऽध्यवसायकरः ।

"Even a slight peculiarity helps to make distinctions") and all very *informing*, again, as said before, but not *satisfying*. The explanations require explanation. In the last chapter of his work, Leuba, after discussing (1) the passive and

(2) the godless religions (as he calls Buddhism and Comte's *Positivism*), and incidentally drawing a distinction between religion and philosophy, says, "we would therefore throw out of our definition any thing which did not include (1) a belief in a great and superior *Psychic Power*—whether personal or not and (2) a *dynamic relation*—formal and organised or otherwise—between man and that Higher Power, tending to the preservation, the increase and *the ennobling of life*...Active Religion may properly be looked upon as that portion of the struggle for life, in which use is made of the Power we have roughly characterised as psychic and superhuman, and for which other adjectives, 'spiritual', 'divine', for instance, are commonly used......The conception of the *Source of Psychic Energy*, without the belief in which no Religion can exist, has undergone very interesting transformations in the course of historical development," as indicated by the words polytheism, monotheism, absolutism. "As belief in a God seems no longer possible, man seeks an impersonal, efficient substitute, belief in which will not mean disloyalty

to *science.* For man will have life, and have it abundantly, and he knows from experience that its sources are not only in meat and drink, but also in 'spiritual faith.' It is this problem which the Comtists, Immanentists, the ethical-culturists, and the mental-scientists are all trying to solve. Any solution will have the right to the name Religion that provides for the preservation and *the perfectioning of life by means of faith in a superhuman psychic Power.*" These are the words with which Leuba concludes his book.

We may note, incidentally, that as the definitions quoted by Leuba at the outset show either "(1) an intellectualistic or (2) an affectivistic bias", to use his own words, so his own view shows (3) an activistic one, as when he says, "will without intelligence may be possible, but intelligence without will is not", or again, that "the will is primal, or, in other words, conscious life is always oriented towards something to be secured or avoided immediately or ultimately"; though no doubt he marks a distinct advance, in referring to all *three* aspects of Consciousness, as Pfleiderer and James also do. While, in the case of most of the definitions of religion, quoted above, one or the other of the two kinds of bias appears plainly, in the case of others it shows through in a more veiled manner, as Leuba illustrates more particularly thus: "Pfleiderer (after saying that will, feeling, and intelligence are necessary and inseparable constituents of Religion) hastens to add 'of course we must recognise that knowing and willing are here (in religion) not ends in themselves, as in science and morality, but rather subordinate to *feeling* as *the real centre* of religious consciousness.' So Guyau, criticising the one-sided formulas of Schleiermacher and Feuerbach, says 'The religious sentiment is primarily no doubt a feeling of dependence. But this feeling of dependence really to give birth to Religion must provoke a reaction, *a desire for deliverance.* Religion is the outcome of an effort to explain all things—physical, metaphysical, moral—by analogies drawn from human society, imaginatively and symbolically considered. In short, it is a universal, sociological, *hypothesis*, mythical in form.' What is this but once more the intellectualistic position ?". Of the third kind of bias, the activistic one, he himself forms an illustration, as said above.

William James, the versatile erratic, brilliant, and yet most kindly-natured and sympathetic philosopher, expresses his mind on the subject of religion thus : "In broadest and most general terms possible, one might say that religious life consists in the *belief* that there is an unseen *order*, and that our Supreme good lies in *harmoniously adjusting* ourselves thereto. This belief and this adjustment are the religious attitude of the soul. In the ordinary sense of the word, however, no attitude is accounted religious unless it be grave and serious ; the trifling, sneering attitude of a Voltaire must be thrown out if we would not strain the ordinary use of language. Moreover, there must be something solemn, serious and tender about any attitude which we denominate Religion. If glad it must not grin or snigger ; if sad, it must not scream or curse. The sallies of a Schopenhauer or a Nietzsche lack the purgatorial note which religious sadness gives forth. And finally we must exclude also the chilling reflections of Marcus Aurelius on the eternal reason, as well as the passionate outcry of Job." J. B. Pratt, a living and able writer on the same subject, in America, defines Religion as man's "attitude towards the determiner of his destiny," and, distinguishing four varieties of this attitude, viz., (i) the traditional, (ii) the rationalistic, (iii) the mystic, and (iv) the practical, recommends, for an ideal life, the due combination of all. This seems to be his latest and most mature view [1] though in his work on *The Psychology of Religious Belief* he seems to lay stress on the element of *Feeling* as the most essential in Religion.

(iii) *Causes of conflict and reconciliation.*

All these quotations and extracts help us to see how, gradually, the chaos of ideas about the nature of Religion is taking shape in the West. Its three essential factors are being re-

[1] As stated in a lecture which he kindly gave, by invitation, to the students of the Central Hindu College, Benares, in December, 1913.

cognised more and more clearly, though now one is emphasised and now another, and many different words are used which however express only different shades of the primary three. These biases of Western students of Religion are, it may be noted in passing, the same in nature as the sectarian conflicts of the exclusive votaries in India of Brahmā, or Vishṇu, or Shiva, respectively, the embodiments of the Principles of Rajas-Action, Saṭṭva-Knowledge, and Ṭamas-Desire. The predominance, in an individual, of one of the three functions of mind, makes his special temperament and its corresponding bias. Let us now proceed to examine what the old view of the Nature of Religion was in and for *Vaiḍika* India, and how *Vaiḍika Ḍharma* as a whole fulfils the conditions expounded by Leuba in his closing words, by recognising the *equal* importance of all three elements, "making no distinction between the prophets", and insisting upon each being given its due share of attention.

(iv) *The significance of Vaiḍika Ḍharma as " Scientific Religion."*

'Scientific Religion'—religion "which will not mean disloyalty to science"—is the ideal goal. But '*Vaiḍika Ḍharma*'—hackneyed phrase as it is, and either meaningless in many mouths to-day, unhappily, or, indeed, possessed of a very narrow and sectarian and ill meaning —is it not the exact equivalent of *Scientific Religion*? Nay, is it not more and better? For *scire* refers more perhaps to *sense*-knowledge, while *viḍ*, *wissere*, *wit*, refers more to intellectual, rational, *thoughtful* knowledge which has systematised, absorbed, and assimilated sense-knowledge. Also, the same root *viḍ*, which means 'to know', or better "to be aware or *conscious*" (as including all three functions, and not merely intellection), also means 'to exist,' indicating thereby at once the primal, basic, essential fact that to *exist* is to be the object of Consciousness, and that Universal Consciousness, संवित्, चेतना, is the Fundamental Reality and the support of the whole universe—its One and Only Ultimate.

सत्तायां विद्यते, ज्ञाने वेत्ति, विंत्ते विभावने ।
विंदते विंदति प्राप्तौ, कारणे वेदयत्यपि ॥

पिताऽहमस्य जगतः माता धाता पितामहः ।
गतिर्भर्त्ता प्रभुः साक्षी निवासः शरणं सुहृत् ॥
प्रभवः प्रलयः स्थानं निधानं बीजमव्ययम् ।
उपद्रष्टाऽनुमंता च भर्त्ता भोक्ता महेश्वरः ॥
परमात्मेति चाप्युक्तो देहेऽस्मिन् पुरुषः परः ॥

Gītā.

"I am, i. e., the Self is, the Generator and Father of this ever-moving world, its nourisher and measure-setting Mother, its fostering Nurse and support, its earliest and most ancient Ancestor, its final resort and the Goal of all its endless movements, its maintainer and Husband, its Refuge, its Friend, its Originator, its Preserver, its winder-up and Destroyer, its Reservoir, its Seed unperishing, its attentive yet ever aloof and detached and reposeful Guide, its Sanctioner, its Enjoyer and its Sufferor—the Supreme Lord of it all—the I that is known as the Paramāṭmā manifesting in and through all living bodies."

(v) *The philological and philosophical fullness of meaning of the word Veḍa.*

Such is the profound implication of the very name Veḍa in the ancient language. वेदयति इति वेदः that which enables men to *know* what *is* and what *is true*, that is Veḍa—an implication of Consciousness which is being approached more and more nearly every day now in the West. Even material science there has recognised that life is not to be explained by the organism, but the organism by life ; that physics will not help us to understand psychics, but psychics physics ; that Matter is not the originator of Consciousness, but rather Consciousness of Matter. The quotation from Prof. Bergson made above is indicative of this trend of modern Western thought. To that may be added here extracts from *Introduction to Science*, (H. U. L. Series) by the distinguished biologist Prof. J. A. Thomson : "The aim of *Science* is the *description* of facts, the aim of *Philosophy* their *interpretation*. There is much need for Metaphysics to function as a sublime Logic, testing the completeness and consistency of scientific description......The terms of scientific description require themselves to be explained......Before problems such as the origin of living creatures upon the earth, the secret of the organism, the relation of soul and body, Science and Philosophy meet. Science offers some contributions to the discussion and must then remain *qua* Science agnostic. To most minds it seems imperative to go on to metaphysical theory, and it is better to do this frankly and deliberately than unconsciously or at random." (p. 166, 167). "Science is for Life, not Life for Science" (p. 251). "We cannot describe *thinking* in physiological terms, still less in physical terms". "*Why* things happen...is no proper question for science ; its sole business is...*how* they happen" (p. 47) *Why* is the business of Metaphysics. "The five great fundamental Sciences are (1) Sociology, (2) *Psychology*, (3) Biology—of the Animate Order ; (4) Physics, and (5) Chemistry—of the purely physical order". (p. 106). It should be remembered here that Sociology is the *Psychology* of groups of *individuals*, *jivāṭmās* ; and Biology is the science of their material tenements. Herbert

Spencer (*Psychology*, I, p. 141) also says:— "The claims of Psychology........are......not smaller but greater than those of any other Science...It is...a double science which, as a whole, is quite *sui generis*"; and (p. 159) "were we compelled to choose between the alternatives of translating (1) mental into physical or (2) physical into mental phenomena, the latter alternative would seem the more acceptable of the two".

All the latest and most approved text-books of Psychology are unanimously laying stress on the fact of the Unity and the unbroken Continuity of Consciousness, its एकता, एकरसता, अखंडता, and giving prominence to the fact that an absolute and simple beginning of it or of any of its three modes is undiscoverable.

नात्मा जजान न मरिष्यति नैधतेऽसौ ।

Bhâgavata.

It is true that, as yet, the majority of these writers occupy the individualistic standpoint (corresponding more or less to the Sānkhya)—has not the whole spirit of Western civilisation been individualistic so far? But the next step, let us hope, will not be very long off—of the *higher* Socialism, the Joint Family of अग्रजन्मा, and अनुजन्मा, in economics, and of *Universalism*, अद्वैतभाव, in Philosophy and Psychology. In the East, Psychology or Aḍhyāṭma Viḍyā, and its crown, and the crown and finality of *all* knowledge, Metaphysics or Brahma Viḍyā, have from time immemorial been recognised as the Supreme Science, the foundation of *all* other sciences. The *Mundaka Upaniṣhaṭ* speaks of Brahma Viḍyā, the Science of the Infinite and Eternal, as सर्वविद्याप्रतिष्ठा, the basis of all the sciences, and the *Brahma Upaniṣhaṭ* as वरिष्ठा, the highest, best and most important, on the principles of which and which alone all the other sciences stand securely, by which alone, "functioning as a sublime Logic," in the words of Prof. Thomson, can they be correlated and co-ordinated consistently and established unshakeably without any further danger of internecine dissensions. The *Gīṭā*, that precious manual of intellectual, ethical and practical wisdom, says:—

अध्यात्मविद्या विद्यानां वादः प्रवदतामहम् ।

"Of all the sciences I am the Science of the Self", subjective or psychological science. And Manu, the Primal Seed and Ancestor of all beings that possess *mind*, the Sun by whose light all other lights shine, whose wisdom all other wise minds share, is also represented as saying :

ध्यानिकं सर्वमेवैतद् यदेतदभिशब्दितम् ।
नह्यनध्यात्मवित्कश्चित् क्रियाफलमुपाश्नुते ॥

"All this world of objects, all that is indicated by the word 'This', it is all made up of *ḍhyāna*, contemplation, made up of the very stuff of the mind, of the very substance of the imagination. It is all held together by the energy of thought and thought alone. He who knoweth not the Science of the Self, he can make no actions fruitful, his actions are verily all purposeless and fruitless, for he knoweth not the purpose and the fruit of life."

The *Nyāya-bhāṣhya*—first steps in Aḍhyāṭma Viḍyā says (I. 1. 2.) :

सेयमान्वीक्षिकी

प्रदीपः सर्वविद्यानामुपायः सर्वकर्मणाम् ।
आश्रयः सर्वधर्माणां विद्योद्देशे प्रकीर्तिता ॥

"This Ānvīkṣhiki (which means *Nyāya* and *Veḍānṭa* is the lamp that lights up all other sciences, is the efficient instrument of all good deeds, is the foundation of all ḍharma-duties—and must be mentioned first and foremost in the count of the sciences".

Kāmanḍakīya Nīṭi also says :—

आन्वीक्षिक्यात्मविद्या स्यादीक्षणात्सुखदुःखयोः ।
ईक्षमाणस्तया तत्त्वं हर्षशोकौ व्युदस्यति ॥

"Ānvīkṣhiki is Āṭma-viḍyā, as the science of *values*, because it examines and determines the nature of pleasure and pain. Understanding thereby the essential nature of the Truth and of all life-values, the soul becomes strong to rise above all elations and depressions".

आत्मानमन्विच्छ । यस्तं वेद स वेदवित्. "Seek the self; know thyself; he who knows It knows the Veḍa"—for one can know another and all others only in so far as he knows himself; and he who does not know the nature of life, the life of the physical self and the psychical self, the science of psycho-physics, Aḍhyāṭma Viḍyā, how can he help on the work of life, of right living, of scientific religion, for himself and others ?

So far the significance of the word *vaiḍika.*

(*vi*) *And of Ḍharma.*

What about *ḍharma* ? Is it the true equivalent of *religion* ? Perhaps not. That word seems to contain only about a third or at most two-thirds of what *ḍharma* contains. The *Mahābhāraṭa*, the *Maṭsya Purāṇa*, and other ancient works say :

धारणाद्धर्ममित्याहुर्धर्मेण विधृताः प्रजाः ।
यः स्याद्धारणसंयुक्तः स धर्म इति निश्चयः ॥
तत्रेष्टप्रापको धर्म आचार्यैरुपदिश्यते ।
अधर्मश्चानिष्टफल आचार्यैर्नोपदिश्यते ॥
धर्मेति धारणे धातुः महत्त्वे चैवमुच्यते ।
आधारणे महत्त्वे वा धर्मः स तु निरुच्यते ॥

Maṭsya Purâna, Ch. 145.

Briefly ' that which holds together all living beings in harmonious order is *ḍharma* '.

The *Nirukta*-view is the same :—

नैरुक्तास्तु धारणाकर्तृयोग्यनियमरूपमर्थं मन्वत
इति धारणौपयिको धर्मशब्दस्यार्थः ।

The *Vaisheshika Sūtras* tell us :—

यतोऽभ्युदयनिःश्रेयससिद्धिः स धर्मः ।

"That which enables us to achieve happiness here and hereafter is Ḍharma."

The *Mīmāmsā Sutras* say :—

चोदनालक्षणोऽर्थः धर्मः ।

"Ḍharma is ordinance, impulsion, command",—the jurisprudent's definition of law. It should be noted however that the word which means 'command' here, also means 'inspiration', the inspiring of some one by the Energy of the Inspiror ; compare its use in the *Gāyaṭrī*. Hence the definition really combines in itself the jurisprudential as well as the revelational and scientific ideas of Ḍharma as comprising Religion, Law and Right-and Duty, also Functional causation. In other words, what is commanded from *within* in the first place and, in the second place, from *without* also *in accordance with* that will of *the Universal which is within ail*, as ascertained by the Elders and Seers of the race or the community—that is Ḍharma.

How put all these ideas together in English ? "*Vaidika Ḍharma*, Ārya and Sanāṭana Ḍharma, is that *scheme*, code, system, method and practice of the Eternal Laws of *right*, righteous, and noble *living*, in all departments of life, gathered together from all the available sciences, physical and superphysical, objective and subjective, Veḍa and Viḍyā—as founded in the very Nature of That which is the Ultimate Source of all psychical as well as physical Power and also Substance and of all Infinite Multiplicity and Fecundity, and which is therefore the most Sacred and Mysterious as well as the most Familiar and Near and Dear—by which scheme of laws human beings as well as all the other denizens of the world, belonging to kingdoms sub-human as well as superhuman, are held together in an organised 'Society', a harmonious and universal order, in such a manner that every member of that 'Society', that world, (Samsāra) has the greatest and the best opportunities given to him of developing his higher nature and of securing thereby the greatest happiness and avoiding the most pain, here as well as hereafter, of achieving all that is meant by worldly prosperity, अभ्युदय, and all that is meant by the Supreme Bliss of Mokṣha, निःश्रेयस, than which there is no higher." Briefly, " Religion, or rather Ḍharma, is a scheme of *right living*, in *all* departments of life, according to the best lights available."

Apparently all that is of truth and value in any of the numerous different definitions and descriptions of ' religion ' quoted, or not quoted, above, is to be found here ; and all their conflicts and inconsistencies reconciled; and also all possible and actual religions of all grades and degrees will be found consciously or unconsciously to answer to some one or more part or parts of this all-embracing definition. Whatsoever any one conceives to be ' right living,' which will bring him happiness here and hereafter and which he regards as ' enjoined on him by something within or without,' that is Ḍharma-religion to and for him.

(vii) *The Etymological significance of the word Religion.*

The word Religion itself is a good word. Etymologically (*re* and *ligare* as well as *legere*) it means that which *spreads out* and again *col-lects* and *ob-liges* and binds together—the same, in fact, as the word ḍharma ; but the ideas (1) of a *complete scheme* of right living that will pervade *all* departments of the so-called worldly as well as the other-worldly and the unworldly life, and of (2) law as an invincible causal relation of infringement of duty and punishment, on the one hand, and fulfilment and reward on the other—these ideas are not present in it, except in germ, at least as the word is now used. But they may gradually grow fully and become attached to it inseparably, as in the case of ḍharma.

(viii) *The main features and factors of Vaiḍika Ḍharma.*

What now are the main features, the broad outlines, of this complete code of life called Vaiḍika Ḍharma, in accordance with which *every* function of life may be and ought to be performed in the scientifico-religious spirit so that the whole of even the most commonplace life becomes sanctified and glorified, the meanest duty is seen to be as important, in its own setting, as the noblest ?.

For these main features, we have to go at once to Adhyāṭma-viḍyā, ·the very heart of Hinḍuism, and indeed of all other faiths—though, it may be, unconsciously and subconsciously, as said before.

The Universal Consciousness, **परमात्मा, ब्रह्म, संवित्, चित्, चेतना, चितिशक्तिः भूमा,** in the *individualised* form of **चित्तम्** or **जीवात्मा,** soul, psyche or mind, manifests *three* aspects or functions. In old Greek philosophy and in later European thought, down to about the middle of the eighteenth century, a bipartite classification of 'mental faculties,' into (1) active and (2) passive or receptive, was in vogue. But since then the tripartite division has been steadily growing in recognition and with the further implication that the three represent not so much separate faculties as inseparable and only distinguishable वृत्ति's, aspects, moods or functions. Very different names have been proposed for the three: intellect, feeling, volition; thought, emotion, conation; will, feeling, intelligence; thinking, feeling, willing; imagination, will, activity; cognition, affection, conation; presentation, attention, feeling; intellection, emotion, will; wisdom, will and love; will, wisdom, activity; will, wisdom, power; reception, affection, action; and so on.

The old names are ज्ञानम्, इच्छा, क्रिया. The last is sometimes varied into कृतिः, प्रयत्नः, etc., expressing different shades. The best English equivalents for these seem to be cognition, desire, action. As to why these words are preferable and how they are justifiable, and how and why the use of the other words mentioned above involves confusion of thought and over-lapping divisions, on the one hand, and the mistake of the non-recognition of even so-called physical *action* as a *psychological* fact, on the other—this is not the place to show. The matter has been discussed elsewhere. In the old Samskṛṭ works, ज्ञानं, इच्छा, क्रिया, are undisputed.

प्रथमा रेखा...सा क्रियाशक्तिः, द्वितीया रेखा सा...इच्छा शक्तिः, तृतीया रेखा...सा ज्ञानशक्तिः,

Kālāgnirudra Upanishat.

स्थिरं चरं च यद्विश्वं सृजतीति विनिश्चयः ।
ज्ञानक्रियाचिकीर्षाभिस्तिसृभिः स्वात्मशक्तिभिः ॥
इच्छाशक्तिर्महेशस्य नित्या कार्यनियामिका ।
ज्ञानशक्तिस्तु तत्कार्यं कारणं करणं तथा ॥
प्रयोजनं च तत्त्वेन बुद्धिरूपाऽध्यवस्यति ।
यथेप्सितं क्रियाशक्तिर्यथाऽध्यवसितं जगत् ।
कल्पयत्यखिलं कार्यं क्षणात्संकल्परूपिणी ॥
Shiva Purāṇa, Vāyu Samhiṭā, Uṭṭara Khanda.

ज्ञानेच्छाक्रियाणां व्यष्टीनां महासरस्वती-महाकाली-महालक्ष्मीरिति नामांतराणि । *Gupṭavatī-Ṭīkā* on the *Ḍurgā Sapṭa-shaṭī.*

रजोगुणः स्मृतो ब्रह्मा विष्णुः सत्त्वगुणात्मकः ।
तमोगुणास्तथारुद्रो निर्गुणःपरमेश्वरः ॥

जानाति, इच्छति, यतते; यद्ध्यायति तदिच्छति, यदिच्छति तत्करोति, यत्करोति तद्भवति, etc., these words and ideas are the common property of all the *Ḍarshanas.* सत्त्वं, तमस्, रजस् are the corresponding names for ज्ञानम्, इच्छा, क्रिया, respectively, in terms of Yoga and Sānkhya (*Yoga Sūṭra*, II, 18, and *Sānkhya Kārikā*, 12-13).

(ix) *The (a) Jñāna (b) Bhakṭi and (c) Karma kāndas.*

Such being the three aspects, functions, factors, constituents, essentials—as one likes to call them—of all life and consciousness, *Vaiḍika Ḍharma* also naturally falls into three departments. They are the Jñāna-kānda, the Bhakṭi-kānda, the Karma-kānda. The summation of all three is Ḍharma in the large sense, or, as some might like to call it, Upāsanā, the *Practice* of Religion, active Religion, though others use *bhakṭi* and *upāsanā* as synonymous. It is true that every religion, high or low, narrow or broad, that has helped the soul of man onwards in any time or clime, more or less clearly or gropingly, shows forth these same three parts. It cannot but, for Āṭma-viḍyā is at the heart of every religion, the most childish or the most sage, as Āṭmā is at the heart of all, whether young or old. The distinction is that in Vaiḍika Ḍharma we have it not only at the heart, but in the head and the limbs also, in full development and manifestation. What elsewhere may be in seed and bud, is here in bloom and fruit; what elsewhere is instinctive, is here deliberate and purposeful, with knowledge of why and how and wherefore. Indeed अस्यैव मात्रामुपजीवन्ति सर्वे. We may well say: यथा सर्वेषां मननानां मन एवैकायतनं, तथा सर्वेषां धर्माणां मानवो धर्म एवैकायतनम् इति। All fires, lamps, lights of high and low degree, are very helpful to man, and none may be belittled—yet it is not wrong to say that the Sun includes them all. Even so, whatever of good there is in any living faith or dead, so far as it is known, is to be found here with its हेतु, its justifying reasons; and very much that is to be found clearly set forth here, is not to be found elsewhere. Most religions have their Ways of Knowledge and Illumination, of Faith and Devotion, and of Works without which Faith is dead—but none other seems to have set them forth in the same deliberately systematic way that *Vaiḍika Ḍharma* expressly does.

Every religion tells its followers; (*a*) what

to know (think or believe); (*b*) what to desire (or feel); (*c*) what to do. But the others do so more or less vaguely. *Vaiḍika Ḍharma* does it explicitly.

(*a*) Every other religion too, includes within itself a body of doctrine relating to the whence, the whither, the how, and the why, of the visible and the invisible worlds, and of the human and other life inhabiting these, which is its answer to the question, what to know? (*b*) Every other religion too again possesses as an integral part, a system of ethics or morality which is its answer to the question, what to feel? And (*c*) finally, every other religion too lays down a more or less elaborate code of sacraments and a general social polity, which is its answer to the question, what to do? But it does so mostly without systematic formulation.

(*a*) The *Vaiḍika Ḍharma*, in its Jñāna-kānda, tells us what are the most essential and valuable facts and laws of the Universe, which have the most important and incessant practical bearing on our life and which it is therefore most useful and necessary for us to know. This is its department of philosophy and science — expounded in the Darshana-Sūṭras or Upāngas, the 'further or deeper organs' of the Vedas, based upon the corresponding portions of these *i.e.*, the Upanishats.

नहि ज्ञानेन सदृशं पवित्रमिह विद्यते ।
सर्वं ज्ञानप्लवेनैव वृजिनं संतरिष्यसि ॥ *Gīṭā*.

"There is no purifier like unto Right Knowledge; with the help of the boat of Right Knowledge may the soul float safely across the tumultuous waves of sin and evil."

(*b*) In its Bhakṭi-kānda, sometimes called the Upāsanā-kānda, it tells us what are the righteous and noble feelings or emotions that we should cultivate towards the Supreme Being within and without us, and towards all our fellow-creatures of high and low degree, in accordance with the knowledge supplied to us by the Jñāna-kānda. This is its department of practical psychology and character-building, of ethics and morality, (usually described as the Science of Conduct, but which should properly be defined as the Science of Feeling, of the Emotions which are the immediate motives and causes of conduct)—expounded in the Bhakṭi-Sūṭras which enlarge in detail upon the corresponding ideas briefly indicated in the Ḍarshanas, and which are connected with the hymns and Sūkṭa manṭras of the Veḍas.

यस्य शुद्धं मनो नास्ति तस्य सर्वाऽफला क्रिया ।
नैष्कर्म्यमप्यच्युतभाववर्जितं
न शोभते ज्ञानमलं निरंजनम् ।
कुतः पुनः शश्वदभद्रमीश्वरे
न चार्पितं कर्म यदप्यकारणम् ॥

Bhāgavaṭa.

"When the mind is not clean and pure, all deeds are fruitless. Even stainless Recognition of the Unmanifest is incomplete without the Spirit of the infinite Compassion; how much more satisfactionless must Action be, which at the best is tainted with some harm to some, however sacrificing it be made, if it be not inspired by aspiration for assonance of the individual will with the Universal".

(*c*) In its Karma-kānda, it tells us what to do in accordance with the righteous feelings evoked by the Bhakṭi-kānda, to purify and elevate and make ever richer and more beautiful the individual as well as the communal life, physical and spiritual, of human beings, in the first place, and of the beings of the other worlds and kingdoms of nature, in the next.

This is its department of Conduct proper, of applied science, especially psycho-physics and sociology as subserved by all the other sciences —expounded in the Shrauṭa, Smārṭa, Gṛhya, and Ḍharma Sūtras related to the Yajña manṭras of the Veḍas.

आचारलक्षणो धर्मः संतस्त्वाचारलक्षणाः ।
आगमानां हि सर्वेषामाचारः श्रेष्ठ उच्यते ॥

Mahābhāraṭa.

"Good conduct is the truest mark of Ḍharma. It is the mark of the good men and the saints. It is even higher and better than all knowledge—so declare the wisest of the inherited traditions".

It is true that human beings, as they show forth more of the one or the other of the three aspects, fall into one or the other of the three classes of ḍvijas, twice-born, expressly recognised by the *Vaidika Dharma*—as by no other religion —men of thought, men of art and feeling, men of action. It is also true that according to the temperament will be the inclination towards the Jñāna-mārga, or the Bhakti-mārga, or the Karma-mārga. Yet the *Vaidika Dharma* makes it clear that the three qualities are inseparable, though one may be, nay, must be, predominant, in any one given individual in any given time, place, and circumstance.

वैशेष्यात्तु तद्वादस्तद्वादः। *Brahma Sūtras*, II. iv. 22.

न तदस्ति पृथिव्यां वा दिवि देवेषु वा पुनः।
सत्वं प्रकृतिजैर्मुक्तं यत्स्यादेभिस्त्रिभिर्गुणैः॥

Gītā.

अन्योऽन्याभिभवाश्रयमिथुनजननवृत्तयश्चगुणाः।

Sānkhya Kārikā, 12.

And it makes clear that the three ways, of right knowledge, right desire, and right action, are not separable from each other, any more than the three aspects of consciousness.

(x) *Their inseparability.*

They are only distinguishable from one another, and all always necessarily co-exist and interweave, all making but One Three-fold Path of त्रिवृद्ब्रह्म which must be trodden by every soul in its passage from the great deep to the great deep of the ineffable bliss and peace of the Divine Life. The danger of trying to separate the three portions of this *triune* path and follow any one only, and wholly abandon the other two, are very great. Mere Knowledge, reasoning, argument, science, unvivified by the living warmth of love, remains essentially incomplete and erroneous and leads ultimately to that deadly lack of interest, that stony coldness of heart, which is a taste of the isolation of Avīchi, the motionless imprisonment of the writhing jinn in the sealed bottles of Solomon. Excessive Devotion, unbalanced, unadjusted, unguided by Reason, always leads, as history shows a thousand times, to unnatural perversions of emotion, to sex-corruption, hysterics, spiritism, unctuous cant, hypocrisy, nervous diseases of mind and body of all kinds; for love must move either upwards, or downwards, and when, in the course of its spirals, it returns from the upward direction and cannot find the consecrated ways of wedlock in its fleshward journey, it perforce finds tortuous and evil ways for its expression, even as a healthy stream of water dammed back from its normal course between its natural banks, and not provided with healthier and more serviceable irrigation-channels overflows the neighbouring lands in harmful ways. Even so, Action uninspired by selfless Love, unguided by Wisdom, becomes either aimless and meaningless mummery and superstition and ritualism, or positive vice and crime, a fever of restlessness and ruthless ambitions. Therefore all religions which are at all complete show forth all three sides; they inspire Action with unselfish Devotion, and guide both by Wisdom. And *Vaiḍika Ḍharma* does this with pre-eminent clearness and insistence.

Such is the general scheme, in broad outline, of the Sanāṭana Ārya *Vaiḍika Ḍharma.* All religions necessarily conform to the triple requirements of the human constitution, no doubt. But it may well be doubted if any other provides for and satisfies them in the same scientific and deliberate manner. Every religion (as indeed every science, in a very closely allied sense) has its *manṭra*, its *ṛshi*, its *devaṭā*, even its *chhanḍas*, and its *viniyoga*, i.e., its revelation or scripture, the seer and messenger of that revelation, the revealing deity, the special and peculiarly appropriate words and tones and arrangements thereof in which the revelation produces results most effectively, and the special occasion, use and application of the revelation. But it may be questioned if any other has them in the same systematic, all-comprehensive, encyclopedic arrangement as the *Veḍas*, the *Upaveḍas*, the *Veḍâṅgas*, the *Veḍopāṅgas*, the *Pañchama-veḍa* or *Iṭihāsa-Purâṇa*, (connected with the *Brāhmaṇa* portion of the Veḍas), *i. e.*, the History of World-Evolution-and-Dissolution, (vide *Chhānḍogya*, III, iv, i, 2; vii, 1, 2, 4, ; ii. i; vii, i; *Bṛhaḍâraṇyaka*, II, iv. 10) and the derivative *Viḍyâs*—all in terms of *viḍ*, knowledge—with their respective seers and revealers, their corresponding greater and lesser gods and nature-forces, and their appropriate uses. Indeed it is doubtful if any of the other religions even endeavors to define religion as has been done in the *Aṅgas*, *Upāṅgas* and *Iṭihāsa-Purāṇa*. By these comparisons no belittlement of any is intended even distantly; rather in utmost humility of spirit we must offer reverence before all lamps that have been ever lighted by any helpers of their fellow-men to enlighten the darkness through which the human soul has groped in any time or clime in its quest for its lost birth-right of the Eternal. Nay, more, we must recognise that in the nights and in the lands when and where the Sun does not shine, these lamps and fires are the only ones that are of avail. Yet also we must offer even greater reverence and homage unto the Sun, from whom these other lights and fires derive their potencies, when we are so fortunate as to behold it in its glory.

II. The Jnāna-kānda, the Science and Philosophy or Rationalism, of Religion.

(i) The Sacred Source of all things and powers, psychical and physical; the One Spirit in many forms.

Under the sub-division of knowledge, (i) every great religion more or less clearly teaches the existence of a Supreme Spirit, a Self-dependant all-pervading Life, binding together all beings in mutual relationship of duty and dependence, named variously as Ahura Mazda, Ahmi, Zerouan Akerane, Osiris, Jehovah, God, Allāh, Khuḍā, etc. The nature of this Universal Spirit, hidden in the heart of every living thing, and yet also patently manifest in all things, is also described in almost the same terms in the crowning teachings of the most thoughtful followers and finest exponents of every such religion, the Pāramiṭā teachings of the Buḍḍha and the Jina to their Arhaṭ disciples, the Gnosis of the Christians, the Ṭasawwuf of Islam. Of it has been declared: "Har che bīnī bi-ḍān ki mazhar-i-ū-st", "Whatsoever thou beholdest know to be but a manifestation of That." Of It the great teachers Shams Ṭabrez and Mansūr declared: "Haq ṭu i" and "An-ul Haq", "Thou art God, the One Truth and Reality," and "I am That same". The great Islamic kalema of faith, "Lā ilāh'l'illah," "There is no other God, no other true Being, or Creator, than the one God," is a declaration of the existence of the same One and supreme Spirit whose name is That (or rather, That-ness, Samskṛṭ Ṭaṭ or Ṭaṭṭvam, which is said to be, in Arabic, the literal meaning of the word Allāh). The Christian teaching also is that "man is the living temple of God" and that "I and my Father are one". But the teaching is more or less germinal; and has been supplemented, by the followers, in various unguided ways, in accordance with the needs of their stages of development, as was unavoidable. The Sacred Fire, the Madonna and Child, the Cross, the Tomb of the Pīr, the Kaābā-temple, are objects of heartfelt and most helpful veneration and worship to millions and millions of human beings, born and bred in the other religions, even though their respective Scriptures make no clear provision for such worship. In the *Vaidika* Scheme express provision is made for the souls of all stages.

अप्सु देवा मनुष्याणां दिवि देवा मनीषिणाम् ।
बालानां काष्ठलोष्ठेषु बुधस्यात्मनि देवता ।
उत्तमा सहजाऽवस्था द्वितीया ध्यानधारणा ।
तृतीया प्रतिमापूजा होमयात्रा चतुर्थिका ॥
अग्नौ क्रियावतो देवो हृदि देवो मनीषिणाम् ।
प्रतिमास्वल्पबुद्धीनां ज्ञानिनां सर्वतः शिव ॥
शिवमात्मनि पश्यंति प्रतिमासु न योगिनः ।
आत्मस्थं ये न पश्यन्ति तीर्थे मार्गन्ति ते शिवम् ॥

Shiva P., Dharma S., Ch. 17.

येऽप्यन्यदेवताभक्ता यजंते श्रद्धयान्विताः ।
तेऽपि मामेव कौंतेय यजंत्यविधिपूर्वकम् ॥
ये यथा मां प्रपद्यंते तांस्तथैव भजाम्यहम् ।
मम वर्त्मानुवर्तंते मनुष्याः पार्थ सर्वशः ॥ *Gītā.*

रुचीनां वैचित्र्याद् ऋजुकुटिलनानापथजुषाम्
नृणामेको गम्यस्त्वमसि पयसामर्णव इव ॥

Mahima-stuti.

आत्मैव देवताः सर्वाः सर्वमात्मन्यवस्थितम् । *Manu.*

इंद्रं मित्रं वरुणमग्निमाहु-
रथो दिव्यः स सुपर्णो गरुत्मान् ।
एकं सद्विप्रा बहुधा वदंति
अग्निं यमं मातरिश्वानमाहुः ॥ *Ṛg. Veda.*

"The souls of the child-stage find their 'source of psychic power', their deities, in images made of matter." Do not many even so-called grown-up people, of the most civilised countries, set their hearts on and make idols of the fleeting toys of this world, this palace or that jewel, this favorite or that pet, this power or that glory, this friend or that mate, and find their motive-force of activity in them, so that if these prosper they prosper, and if these fade they fade away also? "The deities of the next stage of men are in the *waters*,"—the waters which as beneficent Parjanya, cloud and rain, make the abundant harvest possible, which as benignant Gangā, 'ever-going' rivers, bear away visible sin and dirt and bring irrigation and trade and traffic, which as the great Lord of all the rivers, the mighty ocean, Samuḍra, give birth to all forms of Shrī-Lakshmī, which as the bathing ṭīrṭhas cleanse of sin and impurity—literally and patently, do they not, apart from other concomitant benefits of travel and intercourse with the learned? "The deities of the third stage are to be found in the heavens", for where can the glory of the Supreme Source of Power, not only Psychical but Physical, be found manifested in greater plenitude than in the Sunlit, Moonlit, Starlit, Firmament wherein live and move in spacious orbits and vast cycles the *Suras* of that literally most extensive and wide-reaching of Sciences, Jyoṭisham, Astronomy—the visible *Suras* whom we know as Inḍra-Bṛhaspaṭi, Miṭra-Varuṇa, Soma, Buḍha, Bhauma, Shukra, Shanaishchara, Ṭārā, Rāshi-ḍeva, Nakshaṭra-ḍeva, etc., Only finally, "the One Deity of all deities; That Whose Glory is manifested everywhere, is found in his own Self, the Universal Self, by the jīva that has completed cyclic evolution and attained wisdom", for the Self is the Witness, the Support, the Manifestor of all the glories of sun and moon and star and contains them all. "The truly and inherently natural condition of Self-realisation in all Nature, wherein the Self realises Its own all-inclusive nature – that is the highest and the best. The next is that which leads up to the former, viz., the condition of meditation and contemplation of various subsidiary objects. Means to this, in turn, is the use of प्रतीक' s, प्रतिमा' s, symbols, reminders of the Supreme, imaged as Inḍra, Miṭra, Varuṇa, Agṇi, in the Veḍas, and truly manifesting in these various forms in the world-process as the अभिमानी देवता's, ensouling spirits, of nature-forces. And subservient to this, finally, are the processes of *homa*, fragrant, atmosphere-purifying and soul-elevating oblations and offerings to the visible fires, and *yâṭrâ*, travels through distant lands, amidst peoples with different customs and nature-scenes of all varieties, to centres of piety and holy aspiration and religious wisdom, and bathings in the medicinal springs and waters of sacred rivers"–all helping to irradiate and invest the things of the physical, material world with the luminous atmosphere of poetic, idealising tenderness and romance in the midst of science.

Only step by step may the soul rise from grosser to subtler, from outer to inner; only

4

ultimately, after long journeyings, and with much careful tending, not violent hurrying, may it find Itself. "The god of the man of action is in Fire"—witness modern civilisation and its basis on machinery worked by heat. "The god of the man of feeling is in the *hṛṭ* or heart", the *phren* of the Greeks, the manifesting *locus* of all emotions, art, poetry, mystic experience. "The God of the man of knowledge is Everywhere"—witness the 'homeless wanderer', the pari-vrājaka sannyāsi, the lā-makān of the Persian. "The god of the undeveloped mind is in conerete images", by indefeasible law of nature. "They who cannot find Shiva, the Supreme Good, the Final Peace, in their Self, they seek for That outside, in the holy places. The Yogis see It, not in images, but in their Self." The jīva can find its अभीष्ट, its ideal, either inside or outside; there is no third; and the natural process is, first outside, then the Inside which includes the outside.

"Even they that worship minor gods with earnest faith--they also worship only Me in other forms, though these be not the highest laid down by the Scriptures. On many paths mankind are ever searching; on all these paths they search only for Me—their own most inward Universal Self. And howsoever they may search that Self, the Self shall find them all, and they the Self, sooner or later."

"Verily, O Spirit of all! art Thou the Common Goal of all the paths men follow as they variously incline, some straight and easy, others crooked and rough—as of the countless streams the one vast sea. Verily is Āṭmā all the gods at once, and all things are in the Consciousness that is the Self. One is It, yet they call It many ways, Inḍra, Miṭra, Varuṇa, Agni, Suparṇa Garuṭmān, Yama, Māṭarishvā. Indeed all names are names of It alone." Thus all-embracing, none-excluding, thus profoundly true and tender, is the whole Spirit of the *Vaiḍika Ḍharma*.

The *Ārambha-vāḍa*—in the two *Nyāyas*—the *popular* notion of causation, creation of one thing by another, of the world by an extra-cosmical Personal God, as of pots by a potter; the *Pariṇāma-vāḍa*—in the two *Sāṇkhyas*—the *scientific* view of causation—that the world is the product of the blind interplay or motion-transformations of indestructible matter, Prakṛṭi, with unanalysably persistent forces, Purushas; and finally, the *metaphysical* view of causation—the *Vivarṭa-vàḍa*—of the *Mimāmsās*—that the world-process is a *Necessary Illusion*, due to the Māyā-svabhāva, the very Nature, of the Supreme Self, which makes it *appear* to swing between Pravṛṭṭi and Nivṛṭṭi, *āvir-bhāva* and *ṭiro-bhāva*, manifestation and disappearance, *sarga* and *apavarga* —the very heart-beat of the whole Universe;—all these are expounded and included, stage by stage, and grade by grade, in the Religion of Knowledge—*with appropriate modes of worship.* The house wherein there are only the aged—is a house of gloom, lacking light and life, an abode of ghosts; the house wherein there are only children left—is a house of helplessness and quarrelling, lacking wisdom and the management that holds them all together lovingly—a cage of monkeys. That house only is a *home*, where three generations dwell together; the grand-babies with their toys and alphabetic picture-books of symbols and प्रतीक 's, for whose sake and around whom so much beautiful, reverential, glorious Art is gathered; the middle-aged parents with their bread-winning Enterprises and travels and studies and offerings into the fires of various earthly and heavenly ambitions; and, finally, the grand-parents, overflowing with loving Wisdom and holding all together in the all-comprehending Consciousness of the Supreme, and *ever reminding* the younger generations that their playthings—not to be violently and prematurely broken—are yet only passing *play-things*, *means* to something higher, *not to be clung to forever*. The house of the sagest philosopher and scientist is empty without prattling children; and therefore the ancient Scheme of Life deals very tenderly with the ungrown intelligence, and helps it to grow, insistently and yet very gently. Such an *Ideal* Home is the *Vaiḍika Ḍharma*—if only it be duly and reverently understood and followed—providing *spiritual* as well as *material* nourishment *to all possible grades of souls*.

(ii) The Nature of the Material Worlds.

(ii) The next item, in the department of knowledge, is the Material World in contrast with the Spirit described above, and in relation with which the Spirit puts on the triple aspect of Creator, Preserver and Destroyer, and again of Omnipresent, Omniscient and Omnipotent, in correspondence with the three aspects of all Life and Consciousness. All religions necessarily refer to this but they mostly content themselves with general statements about the birth and death of the visible world and about a heaven and a hell beyond. In the Vaiḍika scheme, we find a detailed description of the various sub-divisions of grosser and subtler Matter, of *sṭhūla* and *sūkṣhma* Lokas, Svargas, Narakas and Pāṭālas made of different kinds of elements, fit for the life-play and experiences of *Jīvas* ensouling bodies of corresponding kinds of substance, arranged in infinite Brahmāndas, globes and solar and sidereal systems, in ever larger and larger synthesis, correlated with and reachable in and by other states of consciousness than the one we know as the 'waking' consciousness.

अस्य ब्रह्मांडस्य समंततः स्थितानि एतादृशान्य-
नंतकोटिब्रह्मांडानि सावरणानि ज्वलंति ।

Mahānārāyaṇa Upaniṣhaṭ.

संख्या चेद्रजसामस्ति विश्वानां न कदाचन ।
प्रतिविश्वेषु संत्येव ब्रह्माविष्णुशिवादयः ॥

Devī Bhāgavata.

"Around our world-system blaze countless millions of similar brahmāndas in their 'envelopes' (*āvaraṇas*, litho-, hydro-, photo-, atmo-, etc., *spheres*). Grains of sand may be counted, world-systems may not be. And each has its three principal presiding Deities of Action, Knowledge and Desire."

And the broad outlines of the most important and outstanding events of the Evolutionary History of this world-system of ours and all its kingdoms in general, and of the Human Race in particular, are also included in the same scheme, for Purāṇa-Iṭihāsa (freed of whatever wrong interpolations there might be) is nothing else than such ancient History, Cosmogenesis and Biology, and Anthropogenesis and Sociology, narrated in interesting story-form, to suit and interest all understandings, by the deeper lessons of which statesmen and all other administrators of the affairs of men should guide their course and endeavor to make future history less sad and more glad.

सर्गश्च प्रतिसर्गश्च वंशो मन्वंतराणि च
वंशानुचरितं चैव पुराणं पंचलक्षणम् ॥
सर्वस्तरतु दुर्गाणि सर्वो भद्राणि पश्यतु ।
सर्वस्सद्बुद्धिमाप्नोतु सर्वस्सर्वत्र नन्दतु ॥
इत्युक्ताः सर्ववेदार्थाः भारते तेन दर्शिताः ।
यतः कोमलबुद्धीनां त्रयी न श्रुतिगोचरा ॥
चकार संहिताश्चान्या व्यासः कृपणवत्सलः ।
प्रवृत्तः सर्वभूतानां हिताय भगवान् सदा ॥
यः स्वानुभावमखिलश्रुतिसारमेक-
मध्यात्मदीपमतितीरषतां तमोऽधम् ।
संसारिणां करुणयाऽह पुराणगुह्यम्
तं व्याससूनुमुपयामि गुरुं मुनीनाम् ॥

Bhāgavaṭa.

"The gradual evolution and differentiation and *vaiṣhamya* of the world-system out of the pralaya-condition; its slow involution, disintegration, dissolution back into primal homogeneity and *sâmya*; the various genera and species, races and kingdoms, of living beings dwelling therein, the manvanṭaras, great cyclic periods of *human* evolution and involution more specifically; and still more specifically, the history of the human races and dynasties and the growth and decay of societies and civilisations—these are dealt with in the *Purāṇa.*"

"That all, even the feeblest, souls may safely cross beyond the difficult and dangerous places of life, that all may see the face of happiness, that all may attain to right and righteous knowledge, that all may rejoice everywhere—for this did the lord Vyāsa, compassioning over the whole of weak humanity as a mother over her one babe, ever tending watchfully with unremitting labour the good of all, put into easy words the most important teachings of the Veḍas; and other works also did he compile for the same purpose. And the youthful son of Vyāsa too in passionate pity for mankind, struggling blindly in the black darknesses of earthly life, placed the light of his whole Spiritual wisdom, the essence of the whole of the Veḍas, of all traditional knowledge and race experience, wherein all ancient secrets are stored away, in the storied oil-vessel of the Purāṇa and made of it a beautiful, attractive, many-colored and refulgent lamp wherewith to dispel the gloom from which the children of Manu were suffering, and so enabled them to cross beyond the turmoils of Rebirth and endless revolutions on the wheel of Life, and win unto the Final Truth." *

वदंति तत्तत्वविदः तत्त्वं यज्ज्ञानमद्वयम् ।
ब्रह्मेति परमात्मेति भगवानिति शब्द्यते ॥

Bhāgavaṭa.

"They who know the Truth declare that the only Truth is the Truth of the secondless Unity of Spirit—known variously as Brahman, Paramāṭmā, Bhagavān."

Without deep knowledge of evolutionary and sociological history no conduct of the affairs of men can be successful. The genuine *Iṭihāsa-Purāṇa* contain all the *essentials* of such history. They only require to be duly elucidated. And they will help to elucidate the Veḍas in turn.

इतिहासपुराणाभ्यां वेदं समुपबृंहयेत् ।
बिभेत्यल्पश्रुताद् वेदो मामयं प्रतारिष्यति ॥

"The Veḍa fears the man of little knowledge: 'he will despoil me of the rightful richness of my meaning.' Therefore the Veḍa should be expounded always with the help of the History of Evolution."

(iii) The countless forms of living beings, composed of Spirit and Matter, dwelling in the Worlds.

(iii) Another common item of belief is the existence of different grades of super-physical beings dwelling in these different worlds, even as men and animals live in this, all within and under the Nature and Law and sway of the One Supreme Spirit which lives and moves in all. Farohars, Elohim, Angels, Cherubs, Seraphs, Sprites, Gnomes, Undines, Salamanders, Sylphs, Dryads, Banshees, Yama--no--Kami, Fairies, Farishṭas, Jinns, Paris, etc.--are the names given by Buḍḍhist, Jain, Sikh, Pārsī, Shintoist, Hebrew, Christian, and Musalmān, to these same spirits, some benevolent, some malevolent to humanity. All religions also believe more or less clearly in special manifestations of the Supreme Principle of Consciousness, distinguishable within but not separable from the general manifestations of life, like a mountain amidst hills, like a sun amidst lesser lights. They call them by various names, Buḍḍhas, Jinas, Ṭīrṭhankaras, Zarḍushṭas,

Sons of God, Rasūls, Messengers, Nabis, Prophets, Saints, Sages, Seers, Poets, Imāms, Messiahs, Bābs, Heroes, Geniuses, etc. etc. Each name has its own special significance of function and degree. But it is perhaps the *Vaiḍika Ḍharma* alone that gives us a full and systematic statement of the sub-human and super-human kingdoms through which the soul evolves and involves, the millions of types, divided into mineral, vegetable, animal, human, ḍeva and other kingdoms, the main types of ḍevas and upaḍevas, yakshas, ganḍharvas, apsaras, pishāchas etc. of good and evil nature (vide *Yoga-Sutra-Bhāshya*, III, 26,) and tells us how man can establish relations with the beneficent and avoid them with the maleficent. It also explains to us how Avatāras, Āveshas, Amshas, Kalâs, Kavis, Ṛṣhis, Maharṣhis, Devarṣhis, Paramarṣhis, of various degrees, are perpetually appearing on all planes of matter, in all worlds, and in all kingdoms, देवतिर्यङ्नृयोनिषु, ḍeva, animal, and human, for their helping, according to a fixed law :—

यदा यदा हि धर्मस्य ग्लानिर्भवति भारत ।
अभ्युत्थानमधर्मस्य तदाऽऽत्मानं सृजाम्यहम् ॥ *Gītā*

The general principle underlying these special manifestations is that the Universal Self appears in them in an intenser form than in others, on special occasions, for special purposes of (a) teaching, (b) of adjusting and chastening, and (c) of leading onwards by inspiring love. But the difference between the special and general manifestations is ever one of degree only, for it is literally true that all living things are the children of God, Spirit of the same Spirit and flesh of the same flesh, are 'Avaṭāras', descents of Spirit into Matter, are compounded of the self-same Spirit and Matter. Looked at thus, the fact of Avaṭāras becomes divested of all sensational mystery and wonder-working and is seen to be only one of the facts of nature, and a fact which is much less overwhelmingly astonishing, if at all, than the daily marvels of sunrise and sunset. A homely illustration may perhaps make plain 'the mode of operation' of the Principle of Consciousness in such manifestations. In the case of a human individual, when a thorn pierces his foot, while the general vital consciousness pervading and upholding the whole of his body is by no means wholly drawn away from all other parts but continues to nourish them, yet there is a special concentration of it at the point where the thorn is rankling, and another corresponding concentration in the hand which, guided by the principle of knowledge (Vishṇu), travels to that point to remove the cause of the pain. Even so, in the life of a nation, a race, a group-soul, when Sin, Evil, Aḍharma, Praṭi-nārāyaṇa, the spirit of Negation of the Self, Satan, Kāma-Kroḍha, the Matter-ward tendency, Egoism, Ahaṅkāra, becomes excessive, and concentrated in some jīvas, Rāvaṇa, Mahisha, Ḍuryoḍhana, etc. then some soul, embodying in an especial degree the principle of Ḍharma-Virtue, appears to apply the remedy. Avaṭāras come to show the way, to erecṭ a standard, to set an example, to be imitated with effort and striving; they do not come in order to be blindly worshipped. Indeed, many have had occasion expressly to forbid such blind worship of themselves, as tending to retard the Realisation of the Great Self which is the end, Avaṭāras being but means.

(iv) The Nature of the Evolution and Involution of these living beings.

(iv) All religions also indicate that the human soul, being a portion of the Divine Being, has emanated from It and will go back to It some day, after passing through various experiences of good and ill, virtues and joys, sins and sufferings, in various worlds. But systematic and detailed teachings on this periodical descent and reascent of Spirit, Pravṛṭṭi and Nivṛṭṭi, (which, supplementing physical science with superphysical, and material evolution with psychical, and both with the opposite processes of dissolution or *prati-prasava*, it calls पुनर्जन्म, संसरण, etc., or Rebirth) and the laws governing this evolution and involution of soul and body, through various stages and kingdoms of nature, in birth after birth, are to be found perhaps only in the *Vaiḍika Ḍharma.* Only echoes and reflections thereof, mostly faint, may be observed in the mystic traditions and teachings of other great living religions, sometimes preserved secret as Ilm-i-sīnā, in the 'hearts' and memories of teachers and disciples, and seldom published broadcast, elsewhere than in Hinḍūdom, because perhaps elsewhere the masses were not ready to receive them for lack of the needed spiritual atmosphere and for prevalence of a more worldly tendency.

One fact ought to be emphasised here, *viz.*, this :—

The notion of Evolution is utterly incomplete without the notion of a corresponding Involution; and, again, the dual notion of the two as manifesting in the physical tenements, the biological and physiological forms, is utterly incomplete until supplemented by and *co-ordinated* with the corresponding *psychological* phenomena. The subject can obviously not be dwelt on at length here. Briefly, when it is realised, in terms of modern science and philosophy, that what is called the passing of the अनुद्बुद्ध or sub-conscious (or) supra or unconscious, as variously called in the present unsettled state of terminology) into the उद्बुद्ध or conscious is essentially the same thing as is connoted by the word Evolution; and that *per contra*, the passing of the conscious into the sub-conscious is what might be called Involution (or dissolution); then are seen in the Samskṛṭ views on the subject a significance and a value which were greatly hidden before. The व्यक्त, the finite, the definite, the manifest, arising within and out of the अव्यक्त, the unmanifest, the Indefinite, the Infinite; and then sinking back and dissolving into It again; this rhythmic swing which is the life-pulse of the whole World-Process, on all scales and in all departments of nature, is equally true of mental and material, psychical as well as physical, phenomena; better to say, is true of all psychophysical phenomena, for the two aspects go together inseparably. Different sciences, looking at one and the self-same fact from different standpoints, give different names to the countless pairs of opposites which express its endless aspects. Thus the Sāṅkhya speaks of वैषम्यम् and साम्यम्, heterogeneity and homogeneity, as conditions of manifestation and dissolution; of विकृतिः and प्रकृतिः, specific products and generic root-matter; of आविर्भाव and तिरोभाव, patency and latency, appearance and disappearance ; of ईहा and उपरम, the will to live in various ways, and the resignation thereof. The Yoga speaks of अभिव्यक्ति and

प्रतिप्रसव, the gradual development, definition, demarcation, differentiation of attributes, and their blurring and return to the seed and germ condition ; of व्युत्थान and निरोध, reminiscence and obliviscence, the exhibitive and the inhibitive moods of mind ; of अविद्या and ख्याति, Primal Error and True Knowledge. The Vaisheshika speaks of विशेषः, the principle of singularity, particularity or individuality, and of सामान्यम्, the principle of Universality ; in other words, of the concrete and the abstract. Ethics and Mimāmsā deal with क्रिया and प्रतिक्रिया, action ând reaction ; प्रवृत्तिः and निवृत्तिः, pursuit and retirement; कर्म and नैष्कर्म्यम्, selfish activity and sacrificial activity; कामः and नैष्काम्यम्, the desire to take which binds, and the desire to give and repay which frees ; अभ्युदयः and निःश्रेयसं, worldly prosperity and Spiritual Peace. The Vedānṭa describes the nature of the world-play as अध्यारोप and अपवाद, the hypothetical imposition, i.e., illusory imputation, of endless successive false limitations and forms upon and to the ever formless and pure Spirit, and the refutation and striking away thereof—which is the real significance and explanation of जननम् and मरणम्, birth and death; as रागः and वैराग्यम्, appetite for selfish experience and revulsion therefrom; as अविद्या and विद्या, falling into error and rising out of it; as बंधः and मोक्षः, the bondage and the freedom of the soul. The Purāṇas speak of the same thing in terms of सर्गः and प्रतिसर्गः, Emanation and Withdrawal, आरोहः and अवारोहः, ascent and descent, उत्कर्षः and अपकर्षः, elevation and decline. And every other science has its own special names for them. Yet they all represent only different aspects of the same fact—the māyāvika, i. e., actual yet illusory, diastole and systole of the One Universal Heart which is ever at rest—the *moveless* play of Consciousness (Spirit *plus* Matter), in cognition, desire and action, in substance, attribute and vibration—of Consciousness which is the Unknowable by any "other", but which ever knows Itself as the Self and as no "other" knowable.

(*v*) *The Law of Karma governing this Evolution-Involution in general and the Law of Sacrifice governing human progress in especial.*

(v) Finally, the main law governing all

this to-and-fro is accepted by all religions to be the law of moral and psychical as well as physical Causation or Action and Reaction: As Ye sow thus shall ye reap; *sazā* and *jazā*; virtue is rewarded in the end and vice punished; the wages of merit are joys, the wages of sin, suffering. But it is only the *Vaiḍika Ḍharma* that explicitly formulates the Law of Karma as the law that guides rebirth and evolution and gives us the detailed information needed to enable us to understand its workings in world after world.

तद्यथा पेशस्कारी पेशसो मात्रामुपादायान्यन्नवतरं कल्याणतरं रूपं तनुत एवमेवायमात्मेदं शरीरं निहत्याविद्यां गमयित्वाऽन्यन्नवतरं कल्याणतरं रूपं तनुते ॥ *Bṛhaḍāraṇyaka.*

भूतेषु वीरुद्भ्य उदुत्तमा ये
सरीसृपास्तेषु सबोधनिष्ठाः ।
ततो मनुष्याः प्रमथास्ततोऽपि
गंधर्वसिद्धा विबुधानुगा ये ।
देवासुरेभ्यो मघवत्प्रधाना
दक्षादयो ब्रह्मसुतास्तु तेषाम् ॥ *Bhāgavaṭa.*

उद्भिज्जाः स्थावराः सर्वे बीजकांडप्ररोहिणः ।
स्वेदजं दंशमशकं यूकामक्षिकमत्कुणम् ॥

अण्डजाः पक्षिणः सर्पाः नक्रा मत्स्याश्च कच्छपाः
पशवश्च मृगाश्चैव मनुष्याश्च जरायुजाः॥ *Manu.*

एकविंशतिलक्षाणि प्रत्येकं परिकीर्त्तिताः।
एतेषु भ्रमणं कृत्वा द्विजत्वमुपजायते॥

Garuda Purāṇa.

अचैतन्यं न विद्यते। *Mbh., Shānṭi, ch. 184.*

ओषधिवनस्पतिषु हि रसो दृश्यते।
चित्तं प्राणभृत्सु। प्राणभृत्स्वेवाविस्तरामात्मा।
पुरुषेष्वेवाविस्तरामात्मा। *Aiṭareya Brāhmaṇa.*

परमात्मनः सर्वेऽपि पदार्था आविर्भावोपाधयः।
...श्वासरूपप्राणधारिणः...अतिशयेनाविर्भाव-
स्थानम्॥ *Sāyaṇa.*

स्वकर्मणा सर्वसिद्धिममरत्वं लभेद् ध्रुवम्।
सुरत्वं च मनुत्वं च राजेन्द्रत्वं लभेन्नरः॥
कर्मणेन्द्रो भवेज्जीवो ब्रह्मपुत्रः स्वकर्मणा।
कर्मणा च शिवत्वं च गणेशत्वं तथैव च॥

Devi Bhāgavaṭa.

"Even as a goldsmith breaks up old and worn-out ornaments and makes new ones, even so does the Āṭmā make new bodies. Those that multiply by fission are the simplest; then come those that multiply by gemmation; then the oviparous; then the viviparous. Higher than the vegetables are the animals; than these, men; than men, the pramaṭhas; then ganḍharvas, siḍḍhas, ḍevas and asuras, then the 'sons of Brahmā'. All things and beings whatsoever are vehicles, instruments, media, for the manifestation of the Paramāṭmā. The manifestation is fuller in the higher kingdoms. After working through the lower, the soul evolves into the higher forms. It attains deliberate self-consciousness at the human stage. By its own deeds and efforts it may become a god, a Manu, an Inḍra, a Brahmā, a Viṣhṇu, a Shīva, a Gaṇesha."

In such verses as these we have the plain statement that by appropriate karma, deeds of merit and high aspiration, the soul gradually evolves upwards from the lowest living forms to the highest. That it may delay its progress, or even fall backwards by evil deeds of sin and vice, is also made amply clear in the scriptures. And hence, sacrificial action, yajña-karma, deeds of unselfishness, are especially ordained for the soul that has attained the human stage, the stage of self-consciousness and regeneracy.

सहयज्ञाः प्रजाः सृष्ट्वा पुरोवाच प्रजापतिः ।
अनेन प्रसविष्यध्वमेष वोऽस्त्विष्टकामधुक् ॥
देवान् भावयतानेन ते देवा भावयन्तु वः ।
परस्परं भावयंतः श्रेयः परमवाप्स्यथ ॥
द्रव्ययज्ञास्तपोयज्ञा योगयज्ञास्तथाऽपरे ।
स्वाध्यायज्ञानयज्ञाश्च यतयः संशितव्रताः ॥
एवं बहुविधा यज्ञा वितता ब्रह्मणो मुखे ।
श्रेयान् द्रव्यमयाद् यज्ञाद् ज्ञानयज्ञः परंतप ॥
नहि ज्ञानेन सदृशं पवित्रमिह विद्यते ।
नाऽयं लोकोऽस्त्ययज्ञस्य कुतोऽन्यः कुरुसत्तम ॥

"The Lord of all creatures created them by and together with sacrifice, and enjoined them to live and thrive by sacrifice, by self-denying unselfishness, by the subordination of private to public interests. The race of gods and the race of men can help each other in this wise, and this wise only. Many are the forms in which self-denying sacrifice may be performed. But the sacrifices of knowledge, the sacrifices undergone for the acquisition and the spreading of all true science, *Veḍa* in the most comprehensive sense and especially the Science of the Self, are higher than all other sacrifices. Without the continual self-denial that is involved in that co-operation on which alone society is based, the successes of even this world are not possible to achieve, much less those of others".

Such in very brief outline, are the life-illumining contents of the *Jñāna-kānda* of the *Vaiḍika-Ḍharma*.

Next comes the *Upāsanā-kānda*.

II. THE BHAKTI KĀNDA, THE ETHICS AND MORALS OR MYSTICISM OF RELIGION.

(*i*) *The nature and the use of the Emotional part of Religion.*

The second part of Religion, dealing with the question, 'What to feel?,' is that on which all religions may be said to be almost unanimously agreed. All religions teach us (a) to feel love for all, (b) to be truthful always in thought, word and deed, and (c) to help and serve others. This is the whole essence of morality. And morality, the spirit of Loving Righteousness, is the very heart of Religion, as True Knowledge, Science and Philosophy, is its head, and Performance of Duty, of deeds of merit, its limbs. Without this spirit of Loving Righteousness, religion were like a body without a beating heart, dead and putrefying and spreading corruption all round.

A high 'civilisation', being but a manifestation of a full life in the collective form and therefore of a high religion, in the broad and comprehensive sense of the term, is naturally made up of the same three factors. It is built up (a) of great stores of knowledge, of all kinds of science, physical, superphysical, and metaphysical, (b) of active industries and energetic enterprises ; and, even more vitally important than these, (c) of high morals and purity in art. Genuine civilisation and high culture might perhaps be reached with the help of scrupulous morality and fine or spiritual (as distinguished from sensual and vile) art, which always subserves the highest and the noblest desires and emotions of love and devotion and patriotism and heroic courage, even without much science and without much mercantile and mechanical enterprise, as witness the classic days of Greece. But without these, and even with much science and machinery, we can only have results like those attending the sudden finding of heavy nuggets of gold by rude miners, viz., drunken carousals and shootings. Without this inmost spirit of religion, without high-minded and spiritual earnestness and purity of character, without benevolence and charitableness and philanthropy, no nation can attain to genuine and lasting civilisation, but at most only to that great and passing display of brass and iron and silver and gold which history associates with 'barbaric splendor', be the forms taken those of morion and hauberk and lance and sword, or be they guns and cannon and armored trains and iron-clad men-of-war.

Indeed, the whole of history, the whole of political science, is but a perpetual illustration of the truths and principles of moral psychology. The only permanent use of the former is to drive home the lessons of the latter. The eighteen *Purāṇas* form only an exposition of the consequences of virtue and vice, of Error and its Expiation and Redemption on all scales, individual, racial, cosmic, in all kingdoms, animal, human, divine.

अष्टादशपुराणेषु व्यासस्य वचनद्वयम् ।
परोपकारः पुण्याय पापाय परपीडनम् ।
ईश्वरैरपि भोक्तव्यं कृतं कर्म शुभाशुभम् ॥

Pride goeth before a fall; in the nation as well as the individual, for the plain reason that arrogance estranges friends and creates enemies. Honesty is the best policy, for nations as well as individuals, because honesty is born of that sympathy which feels the Divine Life in all, and therefore instinctively wishes to do to another as it would be done by, and sympathy produces sympathy and converts enemies into friends. Frankness is the deepest diplomacy, for individuals as well as nations, because frankness inspires equal frankness and confidence in the long run, and where there is confidence there is no further room or need for that endeavor to circumvent, which is the currently understood meaning of the word 'diplomacy.' They who promote strife between others, be they individuals or races, thinking to benefit themselves by the policy of 'divide and rule', generally find themselves unable later on to control the evil spirit of strife when fully aroused, and come in for blows from both sides impartially; or find that that spirit, so diligently invoked by them, has ultimately invaded and taken lodgment within their own families and homes and created unquenchable internal dissensions. Hatred ceaseth never by hatred, between men as between nations, though it may possibly be driven underground temporarily by superior might and so compelled to bide its time—but it ceaseth wholly and only by love. Righteousness must prevail in the end between men and between nations, because it makes all loving to each other, and in such a condition of things only is permanence, and not in intrigues and diplomacies. Blessed are the peacemakers only, who studiously promote love and peace all round, amongst all, within their own homes, as well as within and between all other homes; only theirs is the kingdom of heaven, and not of heaven only but of this earth also, and permanently.

And all great and genuine and high-minded and far-sighted statesmen, all the world over, therefore engage with all their might in promoting cordiality and removing distrust between the nations, and between the classes within each nation ; in restraining the smart and supercilious word which it is so pleasant to one's pride to utter, but which flings men and nations and races into lifelong bitterness and deadly feuds; and in encouraging the kindly and agreeable speech which makes men help and co-operate with each other. Truly what cometh out of the mouth is far more immediately important than what goeth in (though the latter cannot by any means be neglected), for the fate of nations as of men. And diligent appreciation of each other is far more useful, far more 'paying', in the common phrase, than supercilious or malicious depreciation. Thus only may the evil aspects of the spirit of unrest that moves from time to time over the face of the earth be allayed, and its good aspects brought to a just fruition.

Whatever, then, promotes moral and friendly relations between single individuals, or between collective bodies of such, is of the very essence of Religion, by whatever name it may be called.

Far more necessary than all else is it to promote this Fellow-feeling. This is why the Scriptures of all times and all nations teach continuously: "God is love," "Love your neighbour as yourself," "Achieve humility of heart and earnest righteousness of spirit, and all things else will be added unto you," "Righteousness exalteth a nation". The nations, the races, the religions, that seek to promote unity or harmony as between their own constituents, sub-races and sects, while fostering contempt of and aggression against other nations, races, religions as such, indiscriminately, will never succeed in bringing about the wished-for harmony within their own limits. It is not possible to heat red-hot the half of an iron bar and keep the other half cool at the same time. We cannot foster evil emotions towards 'foreigners' or 'natives', 'whites' or 'blacks', 'browns' or 'yellows', and at the same time permanently develop good emotions towards those within the same fold as ourselves. The spirit of such Universal Religion sarva-sāḍhāraṇa-ḍharma, must pervade all peoples before any one of them can be really happy. And, accordingly, Vaiḍika Ḍharma expressly includes within its fold *all* the *Varṇas* or types of men, by race and color (white, red, brown-yellow and black) as well as by caste or class or vocation (intellectual, militant, industrial or unskilled); and binds them all together, without exception, into one single social organisation of the whole human race, assigning to each its appropriate place with corresponding rights and duties, privileges and responsibilities, in the bonds of fraternal affection, अग्रजन्मा, and अनुजन्मा, elder (in soul evolution) and younger—nay, in the bonds of what is even more than fraternal affection, of *vital organic identity* of "head, arms, trunk and legs."

ब्राह्मणोस्य मुखमासीद् बाहू राजन्यः कृतः ।
ऊरू तदस्य यद्वैश्यः पद्भ्यां शूद्रोऽजायत ॥

Ṛg-veḍa.

To strive thus to bind all beings together, to spread such a Religion of Love, to harmonise all men and all faiths, to establish peace on earth and good-will amongst men, is indeed to do the work of all sovereigns, all statesmen, all diplomatists and politicians and administrators put together, and to it far better than they are doing it to-day. For this is indeed to water the roots; while they are mostly only washing the leaves at best. And this is why the great Teachers and Founders of religion loom so much larger in the instinctive consciousness of humanity than the other kinds of workers, and are accorded divine honors, and regarded pre-eminently as incarnations of the Divine Spirit, special manifestations and messengers of the God of all nations and all religions, while even the greatest men of thought, men of art, and men of action are regarded as but minor characters in the drama of human history.

(ii) *The Foundation and Fundamental Basis of Ethics.*

(a) *Love* —**प्रियम्** (*The Beautiful*).

But while all other religions and their exponents also, more or less, endeavor to spread Love and good-will among men and enjoin on them to "Do unto others as you would be done by," the *Vaiḍika Ḍharma* is perhaps the only one that gives us the golden rule in its fullest form, positive as well as negative, *and also tells us the reason why*, for only that faith which is based firmly on reason is unshakeable, is scientific faith :—

यस्तर्केणानुसंधत्ते स धर्मं वेद नेतरः । *Manu.*

The words in which the Samskṛt Scriptures endeavor to convey the fundamental teaching of Ethics are like these :—

अष्टादशपुराणेषु व्यासस्य वचनद्वयम् ।
परोपकारः पुण्याय पापाय परपीड़नम् ॥
यदन्यैर्विहितं नेच्छेदात्मनः कर्म पूरुषः ।

न तत्परेषु कुर्वीत जानन्नप्रियमात्मनः ॥
यद्यदात्मनि चेच्छेत तत्परस्यापि चिंतयेत् ।
यदन्येषां हितं न स्यादात्मनः कर्म पौरुषम् ।
अपत्रपेत वा येन न तत्कुर्यात्कथंचन ॥

Mahabh., Shanti, Chs. 124 *and* 260.

आत्मवत्सर्वभूतेषु यः पश्यति स पंडितः ।
यस्तु सर्वाणि भूतानि आत्मन्येवानुपश्यति ।
सर्वभूतेषु चात्मानं ततो न विजुगुप्सते ॥
यस्मिन्सर्वाणि भूतानि आत्मैवाभूद्विजानतः ।
तत्र को मोहः कः शोक एकत्वमनुपश्यतः ॥ *Isha.*
सर्वमात्मनि संपश्येत्सच्चासच्च समाहितः ।
सर्वं ह्यात्मनि संपश्यन्नाधर्मे कुरुते मनः ॥
आत्मैव देवताः सर्वाः सर्वमात्मन्यवस्थितम् ।
एवं यः सर्वभूतेषु पश्यत्यात्मानमात्मना ।
स सर्वसमतामेत्य ब्रह्माभ्येति परं पदम् ॥ *Manu.*

Briefly : "Do not do unto others what you do not wish that they should do unto you ; and do unto others as you would that they should do unto you—*because* indeed the others are yourself in Essence. We can understand and know others, their thoughts, their feelings, their requirements, only by carefully examining and knowing ourselves and our own. He only is the true Pandiṭa, man of conscience (pandā) and of knowledge, who *knows* others by himself, as him-Self, and *feels and acts* for others as for himself, as if they were him-Self. He who knows that the self-same Self pervades all living things, he ceases from sin, he ceases from hate, he will not again fall into confusion and despondency." 'God is Love' *because love* is the wish for *union*, and true union is the realisation of the *Unity* of Spirit which underlies all seeming manyness of Matter. Thus is the Veḍānṭa justified of its high title as 'the Crown, the Finality, of all Knowledge'. Its proclamation of अभेदबुद्धि, the Consciousness of non-separateness, is not the idle dream of quibbling visionaries *but the very foundation* of that most practical of all arts and sciences, viz. Ethics ; it is the inner feeling of that of which the outer expression is *co-operation*, which alone makes social existence possible, which alone 'holds together' human and other beings.

(b) Truthfulness—**सत्यम्** *(The True).*

'Truth' is the fundamental virtue, even as Love is, and for the same reason. Both are aspects of अभेदबुद्धि, the Common Consciousness. The one is the intellectual aspect, the other the emotional, even as Self-sacrifice or Unselfishness is the third or actional aspect of one and the same Great Fact, and may equally well be called the fundamental virtue. In Knowledge, the One Truth of all truths is the Unity of the Self; that same Truth in Emotion is Universal Love; that same Truth in Action is Self-Sacrifice.

सत्यं नामाव्ययं नित्यमविकारि तथैव च ।
सर्वधर्माविरुद्धेन योगेनैतदवाप्यते ॥
सत्यं सत्सु सदा धर्मः सत्यं धर्मः सनातनः ।
सत्यमेव नमस्येत सत्यं हि परमा गतिः ॥
सत्यं धर्मस्तपो योगः सत्यं ब्रह्म सनातनम् ।
सत्यं यज्ञः परः प्रोक्तः सर्वं सत्ये प्रतिष्ठितम् ॥
सत्यं च समता चैव दमश्चैव न संशयः ।
अमात्सर्यं क्षमा चैव ह्रीस्तितिक्षाऽनसूयता ।
त्यागो ध्यानमथार्यत्वं धृतिश्च सततं दया ।
अहिंसा चैव राजेंद्र सत्याकारास्त्रयोदश ॥

On the other hand, and *per contra* :—

असत्याद् भवति क्रोधः कामो वा भरतर्षभ ।
शोकमोहौ विधित्सा च परासुत्वं तथैव च ।

लोभो मात्सर्यमीर्ष्या च कुत्साऽसूयाऽकृपा भयम् ।
त्रयोदशैतेऽतिबलाः शत्रवः प्राणिनां स्मृताः ॥

Mahabh : Anush : ch. 162, *and Shanti, ch.* 33

Briefly : "Brahman is the One truth, unperishing, eternal, unchanging, realisable only by that steady Yoga which leaves no duties undischarged and sets itself not in opposition to any ḍharma. Thirteen principal virtues, truthfulness, same-sighted impartiality, self-control, toleration, forgiveness, modesty, patience, absence of jealousy, generosity, thoughtfulness, noble magnanimity, gentle firmness, and compassion for the weak are but forms of truth. So the thirteen opposite vices, anger, lust, lamentation and vain repining, confusion and clinging obstinacy, restless ambitions, indolence, greed, intolerance, jealousy, superciliousness, faultfinding, cruelty and fear are but forms of the primal untruth and error which forgets the essential Unity of all selves, and regards fellow-creatures as *others* ".

(*c*) *Unselfish Service*—हितम् *(The Good).*

Unselfish service of others and performance

of duty under all circumstances is a fundamental virtue because it is only the external expression of the internal realisation of the One Truth of the Unity of all Life, and of the consequent feeling of Universal Love.

येनकेन प्रकारेण यस्य कस्यापि जंतुनः ।
संतोषं जनयेद् धीमान्स्तद्देवेश्वरपूजनम् ॥
भूतप्रियहितेहा च धर्मोऽयं सार्ववर्णिकः ॥

Bhāgavaṭa. XI, ch. 17.

एवं सर्वेषु भूतेषु भक्तिरव्यभिचारिणी ।
कर्त्तव्या पंडितैर्ज्ञात्वा सर्वभूतमयं हरिम् ॥

Vishṇu Purāṇa.

"To minister to the happiness of any fellow-creature, in any way—this is the truest worship of the all-pervading God, (ईश्वरः, यः ईशत ईशनीभिः, (*Aṭharva-shiras*). The wise man realising that the Self (हरति दुःखम् मृत्युं शोकं अज्ञानं बंधम् इति हरिः आत्मा आनंदमयः नित्यः शुद्धो बुद्धो मुक्तः) pervades and embraces all beings, offers undeviating *bhakṭi* and devotion *to all beings*".

Such is the essential teaching, such the fundamental basis and foundation of the *Bhakṭi Kānda* of the *Vaiḍika Ḍharma.* Only he who *realises knowledge* in *action* has achieved fully that *purity* of mind which is the aim of the *Bhakṭi Kānda* and of the first as well as the last steps of Yoga :—

आमृत्योराचरेच्छौचं भावदुष्टो न शुध्यति ।
तीर्थस्नानैस्तपोभिर्वा दुष्टात्मा नैव शुध्यति ॥
श्वदृतिः क्षालिता तोर्थे किं शुद्धिमधिगच्छति ॥

गंगादितीर्थेषु वसंति मत्स्या
देवालये पक्षिगणाश्च नित्यं ।
भावोज्झितास्ते न फलं लभंते
तीर्थावगाहाच्च तथैव दानात् ॥

Shiva P., Ḍharma S., ch. 17.

iii) *The kinds and sub-divisions of Bhakṭi.*

Further, in the Vaiḍika Scheme, we find statements of the principles of a classification of the modes and sub-divisions of Bhakṭi or Love and of its opposite, Ḍroha or Hate, which enable us to form a science and art of practical mind-purification and character-building such as are not observable in other religions, nor indeed, as yet, in even the most advanced text-books on psychology that have so far appeared in the west. The various emotions, good and bad, are mentioned more or less pell-mell, and virtues and vices are given in lists without any clear attempt to connect them with feelings, in the other scriptures and in the modern western works on subjective science. In the Vaiḍika works it is otherwise.

इष्टविषये बुद्धिः सुखबुद्धिरनिष्टविषये बुद्धिः
दुःखबुद्धिः । *Sarvasāra Upanishat.*

इच्छा द्वेषः सुखं दुःखं संघातश्चेतना धृतिः ।
एतत्क्षेत्रं समासेन सविकारमुदाहृतम् ।
काम एष क्रोध एष रजोगुणसमुद्भवः ॥
इंद्रियस्येंद्रियस्यार्थे रागद्वेषौ व्यवस्थितौ ॥

Gīṭā

अशुद्धिः परपीडा च स्वर्गमोक्षपरिग्रहः ।
स्नेहवैराणि येनेह भवंति स मनोभवः ॥

Shiva P., Ḍharma S., ch. 8.

अकामस्य क्रिया काचिद्दृश्यते नेह कर्हिचित्
यद्यद्धि कुरुते किंचित्तत्तत्कामस्य चेष्टितम् ॥

Manu.

सुखानुशयी रागः ॥ दुःखानुशयी द्वेषः ॥

Yoga Sūṭra.

सुखाद्रागः ॥ दुःखाद् द्वेषः ॥

Vaisheshika Sūṭra and Upaskāra.

तत्त्रैराश्यं रागद्वेषमोहार्थान्तरभावात् ॥

Nyāya Sūtra.

मैत्रीकरुणामुदितोपेक्षाणां सुखदुःखपुण्या-
पुण्यविषयाणां भावनातश्चित्तप्रसादनम् ॥

Yoga Sūtra.

गुणाधिकान्मुदं लिप्सेदनुक्रोशं गुणाधमात् ।
मैत्रीं समानादन्विच्छेन्न तापैरभिभूयते ॥
महतां बहुमानेन दीनानामनुकम्पया ।
मैत्र्या चैवात्मतुल्येषु यमेन नियमेन च ॥

Bhāgavata.

सर्वभूतेषु यः पश्येद्भगवद्भावमात्मनः ।
भूतानि भगवत्यात्मन्येष भागवतोत्तमः ॥
ईश्वरे तदधीनेषु बालिशेषु द्विषत्सु च ।
प्रेममैत्रीकृपोपेक्षा यः करोति स मध्यमः ॥
अर्चायामेव हरये पूजां यः श्रद्धयेहते ।
न तद्भक्तेषु चान्येषु स भक्तः प्राकृतः स्मृतः ॥
गोत्रजः सहजशत्रुरित्यसौ
नीतिरस्तु धनलोभदुर्धियाम् ।
वृद्धतुल्यलघुपुंवृतं जगद्
धीधनस्य पितृमित्रपुत्रवत् ॥ *Bāla Bhārata.*

परोत्कर्षाऽसहिष्णुत्वं स्पर्धा चैव समैश्च तैः
कनिष्ठेषु च संतोषो यावत्पुण्यक्षयो भवेत् ॥

इत्यादि (गुण) दोषाश्च स्वर्गे राजन्नवास्थिताः ॥

Yoga Vāsishtha.

रागपक्षः कामो मत्सरः स्पृहा तृष्णा लोभ इति ।
द्वेषपक्षः क्रोध ईर्ष्या असूया द्रोहोऽमर्ष इति ॥

Nyāya Bhāshya.

Briefly, the purport of the above is that "Desire, इच्छा, or काम, or मनोभव, which is the motive of all action, has two main forms, *viz.*, Love, which goes with pleasure, and Hate, which goes with pain. This pair is called इच्छाद्वेषौ, कामक्रोधौ, स्नेहवैरे, but most often रागद्वेषौ. Further, with reference to the quality of their objects, these two primary emotions take on different forms. Love becomes (a) respect and reverence towards those who are older and greater than we are, and in the highest degree such for our own Inmost Spirit, God, the Supreme and Universal Self; (b) sympathy and affection for those who are equal to us; and (c) tenderness and pity towards the younger, weaker and smaller; *i. e.*, बहुमान, मैत्री and करुणा respectively. So Hate becomes, respectively, (a) fear, (b) anger (c) scorn, भयं, क्रोधः, अवमानः." Where in the count of the well-known 'six internal enemies', viz., कामः, क्रोधः, लोभः, मोहः मदः, मत्सरः—the first, third and fourth, or lust, greed, and blind clinging, belonging apparently to the side of rāga or love, are also condemned, what is indicated is that these are the क्लिष्टांशः, the evil forms or refuse, of the corresponding higher forms, viz. love, reverence and compassion. So, *per contra*, the other three, on the side of ḍvesha or hate, may also have their own appropriate प्रसादांशः or higher forms, as, for example, a just indignation against wrong-doing, a righteous scorn of all meanness, a noble emulation in good work. Difference of time, place and circumstance, makes all these and other endless differences, the details of which can be learnt by appropriate study of the scriptures, especially the literature of Bhakṭi as expounded by Nāraḍa, Shānḍilya, Svapneshvara, and in the different *Purāṇas*, as also in the works of some of the finer-minded followers of the various schools, of Rāmānuja, Maḍhva, Chaiṭanya and others. But the broad principles are clear.

And the *Yoga Sūṭra* quoted above, as also the *Bhāgavaṭa* verse, tells us clearly that "the purification of the mind, (indispensably necessary to happiness here and hereafter, for the well-being of the community as well as the individual, for the full and healthy development of the powers that belong to the physical body and the physical plane as also the powers that belong to the superphysical bodies, sūkshma shariras and koshas and the superphysical worlds, Bhuvah, Svah, etc.,) is possible only by the cultivation of the three forms of love as specialisations of universal good-will, and of resignation, forbearance, bearing and suffering of wrong, under infliction of it upon oneself," (not upon another, when that other is rightly dependent upon oneself for protection—which is the reconciliation between Kṛṣhna's command "Therefore fight, O Arjuna!", and Christ's teaching "Turn the other cheek!"). All the virtues and all the vices, कल्याणगुण and हीनगुण, गुण and दोष, or सद्गुण and असद्गुण, arise out of and are simply habitualisations of these primary six moods, themselves arising in the ultimate Truth of Unity, the ऋतं-सत्यं-विद्या of अभेदबुद्धि, and the Primal Error and Untruth of Separativeness, the

अनृतं-मिथ्या-अविद्या of भेदबुद्धि.

We may thus see that the Sciences of Vedānṭa, Bhakṭi and Yoga, ultimate-Wisdom, noblest-Emotion, finest-Action, which teach that the Spirit in all is one and the same, that therefore men should love each other, and that so only can they most effectively serve and help each other and raise themselves ever growingly on stepping-stones of their dead selves to higher things of greater and finer faculties and bodies and worlds, are not the vain visions of idle dreamers, but the most practical of all practical studies.

(iv) *The Summum Bonum and the Right and the Wrong.*

Two problems which lie on the borderland between Ethics as defined here, viz., the Science of Feeling, and ethics or morality as defined in western text-books mostly, viz., as the Science of *Conduct*, may be dealt with here in the light of the *Vaiḍika Ḍharma*: (a) What is the *Summum Bonum*, and (b) What is the *Sanction* of morality. Between these two is divided up the question of what is the test, the standard, the determinor, of the Right or Good and the Wrong or Evil. The *Summum Bonum* governs the nature of these two and the *Sanction* compels the performance of the one and the avoidance of the other.

(*a*) As regards the Summum Bonum, the greatest good, the highest ideal, the most desirable object or state, the परमश्रेयः, the अत्यंताभीष्टं, all conflicts are abated, all possible views are reconciled, in the *Vaiḍika Ḍharma*, by the enunciation of a few plain principles.

अधिकारिभेदाद् धर्मभेदः ।
(देशकालनिमित्तानां कुलजात्यधिकारिणाम् ।
वर्णाश्रमवयोलिंगवित्तानां प्रकृतेस्तथा ।
सम्पदापदवस्थानां भेदैर्धर्मो विभिद्यते ॥)
यस्मिन् देशे काले निमित्ते च यो धर्मोऽनुष्ठीयते
स एव देशकालनिमित्तांतरेष्वधर्मो भवति ।

Shārīraka Bhāshya, III. 1. 25.

चातुर्वर्ण्यं मया सृष्टं गुणकर्मविभागशः ।
श्रेयान् स्वधर्मो विगुणः परधर्मात्स्वनुष्ठितात् ॥

Gīṭā.

सुखाभ्युदयिकं चैव नैःश्रेयसिकमेव च ।
प्रवृत्तं च निवृत्तं च द्विविधं कर्म वैदिकम ॥

प्रवृत्तं कर्म संसेव्य देवानामेति साम्यताम् ।
निवृत्तं सेवमानस्तु भूतान्यत्येति पंच वै ॥
धर्मश्चार्थश्च कामश्च त्रिवर्ग इति तु स्थितिः ।
सर्वं परवशं दुःखं सर्वमात्मवशं सुखम् ।
एतद्विद्यात्समासेन लक्षणं सुखदुःखयोः ॥

Manu.

मोक्षो वा परमं श्रेय आत्यंतिकतयेष्यते॥

Bhāgavata.

धृतिः क्षमा दमोऽस्तेयं शौचमिंद्रियनिग्रहः ।
धीर्विद्या सत्यमक्रोधो दशकं धर्मलक्षणम् ॥
अहिंसा सत्यमस्तेयं शौचमिंद्रियनिग्रहः ।
एतं सामासिकं धर्मं चातुर्वर्ण्येऽब्रवीन्मनुः ॥

Manu.

श्रुतिः स्मृतिः सदाचारः स्वस्य च प्रियमात्मनः ।
एतच्चतुर्विधं प्राहुः साक्षाद्धर्मस्य लक्षणम् ॥
तस्माच्छास्त्रं प्रमाणं ते कार्याकार्यव्यवस्थितौ ।
लोकसंग्रहमेवापि संपश्यन् कर्तुमर्हसि ॥

Gītā.

यद्भूतहितमत्यंतं तत्सत्यमिति नः श्रुतम् ॥

Mbh., Vana, ch. 213.

महाजनो येन गतः स पंथाः ॥ *Mbh.*

अन्यच्छ्रेयोऽन्यदुतैव प्रेयः ॥ *Katha.*

आत्मनस्तु कामाय सर्वं वै प्रियं भवति ।
आत्मानमेव प्रियमुपासीत ॥
एतत्प्रेयः पुत्रात्प्रेयो वित्तात्प्रेयोऽन्यस्मात् ॥

Bṛhaḍāraṇyaka.

अस्मात्सर्वस्मात्प्रियतम आनंदघनं ।

Nṛsimhoṭṭara Ṭāpanī.

विज्ञानमानंदं ब्रह्म । *Bṛhaḍ.*
आनंद आत्मा । *Ṭaiṭṭirīya.*
ज्ञात्वादेवं सर्वपाशापहानिः । *Shveṭa*
सत्यं प्रियहितं च यत् । *Gīṭā.*

भक्तिःपरेशानुभवो विरक्ति-
रन्यत्र चैष त्रिक एककालः ॥
अतः कायमिमं विद्वानविद्याकामकर्मभिः ।
आरब्ध इति नैवास्मिन्प्रतिबुद्धोऽनुषज्जते ॥

Bhāgavaṭa.

ततः क्लेशकर्मनिवृत्तिः ॥ कैवल्यं स्वरूपप्रतिष्ठा ॥

Yoga Sūṭra.

मिथ्याज्ञानाऽपायेऽपवर्गः ॥ तत्त्वज्ञानान्निःश्रेयसम् ॥

Nyāya and Vaisheṣhika Sūṭra.

व्यक्ताव्यक्तज्ञविज्ञानात् ॥ *Sānkhya Kārikā.*

अथातो धर्मजिज्ञासा। धर्मो हि निःश्रेयसेन पुरुषं संयुनक्तीति प्रतिजानीमहे ॥

Mīmāmsā Sūṭra and Bhāṣhya.

मुक्तः प्रतिज्ञानात् ॥ *Brahma Sūṭra.*

The substance of the above texts is briefly this: "The *Summum Bonum* of the child is different from that of the old man. *Worldly joys*, abhyuḍaya, Kāma regulated by Arṭha and Ḍharma, pleasure guarded by profit and duty—this is the first *summum bonum* for the jīva, while it is treading the Path of Pursuit, प्रवृत्तिमार्गः Deliverance from all bonds, Freedom, Emancipation, Beatitude, *Peace*, Rest, Mokṣha, Nisshreyas, Apavarga—this is the final *Summum Bonum*, for the same soul when it has become fatigued with the pursuit of worldly joys. Happiness is the unquestionable aim always, and always too it consists in Self-realisation. The Self is the nearest and dearest. It is Bliss. The feel of Self, Self-dependence, Self-freedom is Happiness; other-dependence, bondage, limitation, is misery." But in the first half of Life the self is realised and happiness found, instinctively and involuntarily, by the *grasping* of outer things of sense because the self regards itself then as identical with the *body*. In the second half, this same is done, consciously and deliberately, by the gradual *giving up* of the sensuous objects, because the Self now knows Itself as NOT-THIS-body, as अनिदंरूपम्, (*Bhāgavaṭa*, X,ii,42,) but, on the contrary, as सोऽहमात्मा ब्रह्म सर्वभूतेषु गूढः तज्जलान् etc., as That Universal and Infinite and Eternal Self and Consciousness which is in all beings, and in which all beings arise, live, and merge back again. The Self is ever the embodiment of Happiness, of Power, of the most Desired Ideal. But in the first half of संसार-life, it is the lower or bodily and individualistic self; in the second, the Universal Self; and to realise oneself as identical with That is the Eternal *Summum Bonum*. The True, the Beautiful, the Good, सत्यं, प्रियं, हितं, are only aspects of It. The true, in respect of knowledge, is the True proper. The True, in respect of desire, is the Beautiful. The True, in respect of action, is the Good. In other words, the object of cognition is the true (as of misunderstanding is the erroneous); of desire, the beautiful (as of aversion, the ugly); of action, the good (as of mischief, the evil). And the Object of the fullest Cognition is the all-Truth, Omniscient, चिन्मयं, परम-सत्यम् (corresponding to सत्त्वम्); of the deepest Desire, the All-Beautiful, Omnipotent, आनंदमयं, परमप्रियम् (corresponding to तमस्); of the greatest Action, the All-Good, Omnipresent, सन्मयं, परमहितम् (corresponding to रजस्)—all aspects of one and the same Self, Brahman. Whence it follows that complete Self-Realisation involves ज्ञानं, भक्तिः, विरक्तिः, (the last as absence of selfish and presence of self-sacrificing action). The opposite triplet is अविद्या-काम-कर्म, untruthful or partial knowledge (half-truths being always falsehoods), selfish desire, and self-seeking action, which reigns on the Path of Pursuit. So far the Summum Bonum.

(*b*) Now as to Right and Wrong.

"As the end varies, so must the means. Morality is relative; duty varies with the time, place and circumstance of the individuals concerned. What is Right for one person to do, may be quite Wrong for another. What is food for one is poison for another. What is sin for an advanced soul, may be permissible, nay, even meritorious, in a younger. The ḍharma-duties of the soul on the Path of Pursuit of worldly joys, *i.e.*, kāma enriched by arṭha and guarded by ḍharma, are different from the ḍharma-duties of the same soul when it has passed on to the Path of Renunciation, *i. e.*, mokṣha. And under each of those two broad distinctions there are minute details and divisions. In cases of doubt, the science of ḍharma-law must be studiously consulted; offhand answers and decisions are not always possible in this any more than in any other science, in respect of minute details. There are certain aims and purposes which are comparatively universal; hence there are certain ḍharmas, rules of manners and morals, which are common also. Patience, forgiveness, control of passions, honesty, purity, control of the senses, cultivation of the intelligence and the open mind, gathering of knowledge, truthfulness, avoidance of anger—these virtues it is the ḍharma-duty of all to develope and practise diligently. But there are differences as regards others, caused by differences of time, place and circumstance. When conflicts of duties and nice questions of law and conscience arise, they must be determined by means of shāstra-science, in the light of:—

श्रुतिः, स्मृतिः, सदाचारः, स्वस्य च प्रियमात्मनः।

the word of the Scripture-statute, of traditional law and legal digests, of precedents, custom and practice, and, finally, of justice, equity, and good conscience; also of considerations of *bhūṭa-hiṭa* and *loka-sangraha*, *i.e.*, *utilitarian* expediency and social organisation and co-operation, and of the views of the *mahā-jana*, *i.e.*, the *majority* of the good and great, the trusted and respected." No one limited and narrow standard can ever suffice to cover exhaustively all the duties connected with the countless possibilities of the Infinite Self which require boundless space and endless time and motion in all ways to manifest themselves fully. But the broad general principles are clear and a living legislation is amply provided for.

With the help of these, all the disputing

exponents of ethics in the West, from Plato and Aristotle downwards, hedonists, perfectionists, intuitionists, empiricists and evolutionists, can be reconciled and each given his proper place ; even as, from the point of view of *Vaiḍika Ḍharma*, as we saw in the preceding section on the *Jñāna Kānda*, all possible views as to the source and origin and nature of the universe and its inhabitants, fetichistic, polytheistic, theistic, deistic, animistic, hylozoistic, pantheistic, monistic, etc., can be reconciled and each assigned to its appropriate place.

(*v*) *The "Sanction" of Morality.*

On the question of the 'sanction', that which gives its binding and compelling force to ḍharma duty, which compels man to do the Right and avoid the Wrong, we are told :

परस्परभयात्केचित् राजदंडभयात्परे ।
यमदंडभयादन्ये पापाः पापं न कुर्वते ॥
सर्वेषामपि चैतेषामात्मदंडः परः स्मृतः ।
यतस्तु सर्वदंडानामात्मा मूलप्रयोजकः ॥ *Mbh.*
भयादस्याग्निस्तपति भयात्तपति सूर्यः ।
भयादिंद्रश्च वायुश्च मृत्युर्धावति पंचमः ॥ *Katha.*

न यमं यम इत्याहुरात्मा वै यम उच्यते ।
आत्मा संयमितो येन यमस्तस्य करोति किम् ॥
सुखस्य दुःखस्य न कोऽपि दाता
परो ददातीति कुबुद्धिरेषा ।
स्वयं कृतं स्वेन फलेन युज्यते
शरीर हे निस्तर यत् त्वया कृतम् ॥

Garuḍa Purāṇa.

आत्मा हि जनयत्येषां कर्मयोगं शरीरिणाम् ॥

Manu.

ईश्वरैरपि भोक्तव्यं कृतं कर्म शुभाशुभम् ।
यत आत्मा हि सर्वेषामंतर्यमतया स्थितः ॥

Padma Purāṇa.

भयानां भयं भीषणं भीषणानां
गतिः प्राणिनां पावनं पावनानाम् ।
महोच्चैःपदानां नियंतृ त्वमेकं
परेषां परं रक्षणं रक्षणानाम् ॥

"(*a*) For fear of each other, (*b*) for fear of the ruler, (*c*) for fear of Yama—do the vicious, the sinful, the criminal, abstain from wrong-doing. But the fear of the Self which ever lives and moves within all is the root and the source of all these other fears." The pain which *one* causes wrongfully to *another*, comes back to him later without fail because the Āṭmā as *Sūṭrāṭmā*, connects and unites the *other* with the *one*, in a community, as surely as It, in its aspect of *Jivāṭmā*, connects and unites the organs in an individual organism, so that if one organ work wrongly and cause pain to another, the pain spreads through the whole body and comes back with interest to the primarily offending organ. For fear of the Self, ultimately, does every organ in an individual organism, and every office-bearer and every other individual in the world-organism, Agni, Sūrya, Inḍra, Vāyu, Mṛṭyu, Yama, etc., does his ordained duty, on pain of unevadable, unavoidable punishment, in accordance with the mathematically exact and infallible Law of Karma, even as in a national organism, a state, every individual and every office-bearer keeps to his duty for fear (or love) of the Communal Soul, the Oversoul of the people as a whole, in which the sovereign authority is ultimately based. This Law of Karma, as said before, being rooted in the Nature of the Self, the all-connect-ing Unity, governs man and god and worm alike ; only in the case of the sub-human kingdoms it works sub-consciously, as action and reaction, while in the human and superhuman it works consciously. The equation is the same, reaction is equal to action, consequence is equal to act, not always immediately, but always certainly, in the long or the short run ; but in the one case, the co-efficient on both sides is 'unconscious.' in the other 'conscious.'

Thus in reference to the 'sanction' also, may all current and conflicting views regarding its nature, social, popular, legal, revelational, scriptural, conscientious, etc., be reconciled.

Modern western science, biology, psychology, sociology, seeing everywhere the "principle of progressive differentiation or specialisation", परिणति, विकृति or अभिव्यक्ति, "that the progress of development is from the general to the special," from सामान्य to विशेष, from the homogeneous to the heterogeneous, सम to विषम, which is all a most excellent and true description of प्रवृत्ति evolution, and as yet only vaguely recognising "that the further we go back, the nearer we approach to a total presentation having the character of one general *Continuum* in which differences are latent", (Ward's *Psychology*)—this science will come into full accord with the *Vaiḍika Ḍharma* only when it fully recognises the other half of the truth, viz., the fact of involution, the regressive obliteration of differences, the return to the general *Continuum* of Pralaya wherein is all Life, by the gradual dissolution and disintegration of separatist and individualised forms. Then will it be possible to see clearly, in the modern counters of thought also, how all differences of laws as well as facts, reals as well as ideals, things as well as thoughts and opinions of all kinds, arise from and lead back to and merge into Āṭmā, the universal immanence of which is the compelling reason for universal *Bhakṭi*.

We shall now pass on to the third and concluding section of our topic, viz., the *Karma Kānda*.

IV. The Karmakanda, the Active Working and Conduct or Practicalism of Religion.

(*i*) *General Principles.*

Right knowledge leads to right desire, and that to right action. The Karma-kānda is thus the fulfilment and fruition of the Jñāna-kānda and the Bhakṭi-kānda.

भूतानां प्राणिनः श्रेष्ठाः प्राणिनां बुद्धिजीविनः ।
कृतबुद्धिषु कर्त्तारः कर्त्तृषु ब्रह्मवेदिनः ॥ *Manu.*

"Amongst beings, those that breathe are higher in evolution than the others; amongst these, they that have developed mind; amongst those that have achieved intelligence, they are the higher who apply their knowledge to action; and, finally, amongst such, they are the highest whose actions are all governed by the constant sense of the unity of all life in the all-pervading nature of the Infinite Brahman-Consciousness."

The whole of the *Bhagavaḍ-Gīṭā* was uttered to Arjuna to induce him *to do his duty*, to fulfil the knowledge of the deepest truths of *Veḍānṭa* by appropriate *action*. So much importance belongs to this idea that one of the main theses of the whole system of *Mīmāmsā* is that all and every knowledge is but a means to action, karma; and the *Veḍānṭa* accepts and endorses the principle, only adding the explanation, to prevent misunderstanding, that there is one, and only one, knowledge—if we may call it knowledge at all—which is not a means to action or to anything else, but is an end in itself, *viz.*, Self-knowledge; and Self-knowledge, as we have seen before, may indeed be equally well called Self-Feeling, or Self-Maintenance.

We see then that the Karma-kānda is Applied Jñāna-kānda and Bhakṭi-kānda in the truest sense, as mechanical enterprises and industries are Applied Science; that Ḍharma-shāsṭra is the *practical* counterpart of that of which Aḍhyāṭma-shāsṭra is the *theoretical* part, Bhakṭi-shāsṭra forming the nexus. It should be noted, that Karma-kānda does not mean only the superphysical and mystical rites and ceremonies which have come to be identified with the word यज्ञ, yajña, "sacrifice." Such excessive narrowing is part of the general degeneration of the life of the people who profess to be governed by Sanāṭana Ḍharma. It is not to be wondered at, though much to be regretted. It is the very way of Nature to be perpetually swinging from extreme to extreme, between action and reaction. Yet the golden mean ought never to be forgotten, ought ever to be kept before the mind as an ideal, as indeed it is kept by Nature—otherwise no return would be possible from either extreme.

आश्रयेन्मध्यमां वृत्तिमति सर्वत्र वर्जयेत् ।

The Spirit, which includes both extremes, is the very *principium* and embodiment of this mean. It is ever मध्यस्थ and कूटस्थ, and causes, from within, the backward swing from each extreme.

In human history, we witness this alternation perpetually. From manure, by laborious cultivation, with the help of the wondrous potency of the seed, to flower and fruit and corn ; then from that, by natural processes of use and consumption and decay, to manure again. Good customs, good laws, good types of civilisation, established with travail by the elders of the race, grow corrupt with lapse of time and of memory of their real significance and virtue; and then have to be renovated, with much pain and sorrow and struggle anew. Thus it has been with the Karma-kānda of the Sanāṭana Ḍharma. Its narrowing had become excessive in the times of the speaker of the *Bhagavaḍ-Gīṭā*, and he led the reaction against this evil as well as against the other evils of the day, as witness his condemnation, in mature age, of too much addiction to ritual and ceremonial (I, 42-46) and his youthful revolt against and abolition of the Inḍra-makha, the annual worship and festival in honor of Inḍra, and his substitution therefor of the cow-cult, something more immediately useful and popularly suitable for an agricultural, domestic and humanist civilisation. Veḍa-Vyāsa also seems to have helped in this same process of reform by his great and benevolent labors in re-editing the Veḍas and the Purāṇas, emphasising the Upanishaṭs and the Jñāna-kānda, writing the 'philosophical' *Brahma-Sūṭras*, and compiling the 'historic' *Mahābhā-raṭa* and the 'devotional' *Bhāgavaṭa*, thereby endeavoring to re-establish the disturbed proportion between the three factors of life; for disease is essentially disturbance of the balance and proportion of the constituent elements, physical or mental, कफ, वात and पित्त or their correspondents, तमस्, रजस् and सत्त्वम् i. e., इच्छा, क्रिया and ज्ञानम्; and remedy is restoration thereof. And the work of these two wondrous contemporaries lasted for some twenty-five hundred years—when again the same narrowing influences came to prevail and again war had to be waged against them by Mahāvira Jina and Gauṭama Buḍḍha, Ashoka and Vikrama, Shankara and Rāmānuja, and others, each working in his own way, some along the line of philosophical teaching, others of politics and history-making, all endeavoring, more or less, to draw the people away from enslavement by the letter which killeth to the Spirit which bestoweth life.

This then is a perennial process. As clothes are to the body, as bodies are to the soul, so words are to the thought. They grow old and ragged, feeble and diseased, hackneyed and perverted, with too long and too much use, and this begins to suffer. They must be washed and cleaned and changed and renewed, that this may work healthily. The important technical words of Sanāṭana Ḍharma seem all to have lost their original broad and liberal, living and elastic, significance ; and they have to be rendered into and interpreted by means of modern counters of thought studiously in order to renovate their usefulness for the daily requirements and purposes of life. As in the time of the *Bhagavaḍ-Gīṭā*, so now again, the word karma has to be restored to its full sense of " all action generally which is required by duty " and the word yajña to that of " all sacrificial activity, all acts of service," in order that the Karma-kānda may resume its sweet reasonableness. In dealing with the technical terms of the Karma-kānda in particular have we to be on our guard, to make sure of the living sense and to avoid narrow and diseased interpretations which have lost all touch with life and usefulness.

It is the business of this Karma-kānda, the third part of religion, to tell us what are the acts most necessary, important and useful to do in order to make the lives of the individual and the community, of each and all, happy, with reference to this world as well as the other.

All religions accordingly have something to say on this point. They prescribe various special processes called rites, ceremonies, sacraments, and also give special directions for the conduct of life, individual and collective. These, in their detail, differ in the different religions given to or grown up amidst different peoples, living in different countries, climates, and conditions, and differing in their psycho-physical requirements. They may, and indeed ought to, vary as much and in the same way as clothes, foods and houses vary in quality, quantity and form, with varying lands and seasons and states of health and personal needs and individual temperaments and idiosyncracies, and the amount of knowledge and skill available for securing and fashioning them. They are of no greater, *but also of no less*, consequence than these. *Some* clothes are necessary to the civilised man; but it is not necessary that they should be of any one particular cut and pattern; while a healthy body is essential under all kinds of clothes. Even so while Loving Wisdom is indispensable, any particular sacrament or ceremonial or form of courtesy or social convention is not absolutely necessary, though *some* there must be. At the same time it may well be that some schemes and codes of ceremonials and ritual are framed with greater science and precision and appropriateness than others.

In the Vaiḍika Ḍharma the topics of Conduct are classified in various ways, with reference to different purposes. (A) In view of the psychical swing of the individual soul between the two poles of Matter and Spirit, worldliness and unworldliness, pursuit of sense-pleasure and retirement therefrom, activity is subdivided into प्रवृत्त and निवृत्त or ambitious and renunciant.

सुखाभ्युदायिकं चैव नैःश्रेयासेकमेव च ।

प्रवृत्तं च निवृत्तं च द्विविधं कर्म वैदिकम् ।

"Karma is of two kinds, (1) one leading to 'rise' in the world, to mundane joys, success, prosperity; (2) the other to the happiness than which there is no greater."

(B) With respect to comparative importance, we have another classification :

नित्यं नैमित्तिकं काम्यं कर्म पुंसामशेषतः ।

"Actions are either (1) the always-incumbant, the daily duties, or (2) such as are due to be done on special occasions and for special reasons, or (3) optional, which a person need perform only if he desires the particular results that are produced by them. Not to perform the first and the second is to fall below the normal average of mental, moral, and physical health and efficiency as an individual and as a social unit; hence to omit them is to incur प्रत्यवाय, "inefficiency, unfitness, going astray, misleading", (अपाय being the opposite of उपाय is "to sin" in the current phrase, which phrase however itself now tends 'to lead astray' from the real significance, because over-hackneyed.

In modern phrasing, no self-respecting man, who knows what he owes to himself and to society, must neglect the discharge of these duties, on pain of losing his status of gentleman, of falling from his high estate of civilised and re-generate being. Such words, belonging to a living language and livingly connected with an extensive literature, are naturally more intelligible and even impressive to the modern man. That आत्मवान् is the fulfilment of all that is only in germ in the word 'self-respecting,' that द्विज contains all that the word 'gentleman' contains as well as the reasons which make a man a gentleman, that पातक connotes the best possible definition of the nature of 'vice,' 'crime,' 'sin'—this is not the place to discuss; but it may be permissible to suggest in passing, as above, that the old words deserve careful and sympathetic study in the light of modern knowledge, by which alone can they now be restored to some of the old fullness of meaning they possessed before they were cut off from their original times, places and circumstances by historical changes.

As regards the third class of actions, not to perform them is only to forego the special benefits which accrue from them ; and, indeed, such foregoing becomes itself a duty for the renunciant.

(C) With reference to human life as a whole, taken in all its aspects and departments, Karma, otherwise called Āchāra, is dealt with under the heads of varṇa and āshrama, the duties of the various castes and of the different stages of life. For practical purposes this is the most current and most important classification and the two others are interwoven with this. So much is this the case that Karma-kānda, or even the whole of Vaiḍika or Sanāṭana or Ārya Ḍharma is frequently designated as the Varṇāshrama Ḍharma.

(ii) Varṇa and Ashrama.

Because every human being has not only an individual but a social life, because he is always *one* of and amidst *many*, because he is born from and owes debts to others, therefore every act of his has a personal as well as a communal aspect. The word self-respect loses all good sense under scrutiny if the self be taken to mean only the personal self—which corresponds with the lower and selfish nature; it has a great meaning when, and only when, the self is understood as the Universal Self—the element of which in the composition of man gives him his higher and un-self-ish nature.

The Āshrama Ḍharma, the code of the *individual* life, which plans that life out systematically, deals with the duties—to which rights are subservient in the ideal scheme, instead of the reverse—of the human being from birth to death, and the orderly development of the soul's finest potentialities, the fulfilment of its highest needs, and its complete evolution and involution. The Varṇa Ḍharma is the code of the *communal* life, which organises the whole of the human race into one coherent society, one joint family, in such a manner as to enable it to achieve its best and highest destinies in the least painful and most happy manner. Because they belong only to different aspects of one and the same life, these two classes of duties are inseparably intermixed and impossible to separate out completely. Yet for purposes of treatment we may take the āshramas, the successive stages of the individual life, first, as meeting the eye of the observer more immediately, and weave into them the vocations of the varṇas, castes, classes, 'colors', in the second place, especially in connection with the second stage of life, that of the 'householder', the 'family-man,' 'the man of business', in which stage the differences of vocation manifest most prominently. The word varṇa is derived from वर्ण, which means to describe, to show forth or to color, and also to cover over; and the vocation of a person is that which *manifests* his inner character and temperament and acts as a proper *covering* or clothing for his soul.

The main principles underlying the Varṇāshrama Dharma and the broad outlines of their details have been attempted to be set forth elsewhere. Here it need only be pointed out in brief that: A (1) the student, (2) the man of family and business, (3) the disinterested publicist, and (4) the renunciant religieux constitute the normal stages, as needs no argument to show, and make up the full and rounded perfection of a well-ordered and complete individual life ; and that : B (1) the man of thought in whom the element of ज्ञान or सत्त्व predominates, (2) the man of action in whom क्रिया or रजस् is developed most, (3) the man of feeling (to which industrial and fine art are allied) in whom इच्छा or तमस् is prominent, and (4) the unskilled laborer in whom the three aspects are as yet all only germinal and none have sprouted forth definitely—together with various permutations and combinations, crosses, adulterations and mixtures, संकर and मिश्रजाति,—constitute the 'limbs and organs' of the social organism, even as the head, the arms, the trunk and the legs make up the living body of the individual, and exhaust between them all the aspects and varieties of the fullest national, communal, social, racial life, in all its departments and institutions —domestic, ceremonial, political, professional, ecclesiastical and industrial—and also help to solve all the problems connected with these. Incidentally, to show how symbols and metaphors have been misinterpreted and distorted and have thus given rise to great abuses, it may be mentioned that the Buḍḍha, in arguing against the *excesses* of *hereditary* caste that had come to prevail in his day, had to say, on one occasion, that, as a fact, human beings of all castes were seen to be born from women in the same way, not some from the head, others from the arms and so on ; which shows that the grand Vaiḍika *metaphorical* words, that "the four castes were born form four parts of the Divine Man," which logically and with deep and comprehensive significance indicate that the functions of the various castes are the same in the social organism as those of the head, etc., in the individual organism, had begun in his time to be explained *literally*.)

ब्रह्मचारी गृहस्थश्च वानप्रस्थो यतिस्तथा ।
एते गृहस्थप्रभवाश्चत्वारः पृथगाश्रमाः ॥
सर्वेऽपि क्रमशस्त्वेते यथाशास्त्रं निषेविताः ।
यथोक्तकारिणं विप्रं नयंति परमां गतिम् ॥
सर्वेषामपि चैतेषाम् वेदश्रुतिविधानतः ।
गृहस्थ उच्यते श्रेष्ठः स त्रीनेतान् बिभर्त्ति हि ॥
ब्राह्मणः क्षत्रियो वैश्यस्त्रयो वर्णा द्विजातयः ।
चतुर्थ एकजातिस्तु शूद्रो नास्ति तु पंचमः ॥

व्यभिचारेण वर्णानामवेद्यावेदनेन च ।
स्वकर्मणां च त्यागेन जायंते वर्णसंकराः ॥

Manu.

"The observer, pursuer, student of the Knowledge of Infinite Brahman; the householder; the dweller in the forest; the ascetic—these are the four stages of life which all take their birth from the second. Served righteously, in their due succession, in accordance with the law, they lead the regenerate soul to the Supreme goal. Of all the men of all the stages, the householder is the eldest and the most to be honored, by the ordinance of the Veḍa, for he supports the three others.

"The Brāhmaṇa, the Kshaṭṭriya, the Vaishya—these are the three re-generate orders; the fourth is the order of the once-born. There is no fifth kind of man. (Every human being, by necessity of nature, falls into one or another of these four classes.) By straying from the right path, by adulterations and mismatings, by neglect and abandonment of duties, arise the mixed castes and classes."

There are endless discussions carried on at

the present day, as to whether 'caste' is determined by 'birth' or by 'deeds', by जन्म or by कर्म. The discussions are not new They are as old as the *Mahābhāraṭa* at least. As usual, egoism, selfish interests, and appurtenant wrong emotions on both sides exacerbate the discussions and lead the parties concerned into extreme views which are necessarily wrong, on either side, the truth lying always in the mean between the two extremes and being made up of a judicious mixture of elements from both.. The main principles, which ought to govern the decision and the practice, but which unfortunately are prevented from doing so by the passionate animus above referred to, are sunclear and have been stated unmistakeably in the scriptures.

Vāyu.

वर्णाश्रमव्यवस्थाश्च न तदाऽसन् न संकरः ।
न विशेषोऽस्ति वर्णानां सर्वं ब्राह्ममिदं जगत् ।
ब्राह्मणाः पूर्वसृष्टा हि कर्मभिर्वर्णतां गताः ॥

Mbh., Shānṭi, ch. 186.

शूद्रेण हि समस्तावद् यावद्वेदे न जायते ।
जन्मना जायते शूद्रस्संस्काराद् द्विज उच्यते ॥

मातुरग्रेऽधिजननं द्वितीयं मौञ्जिबंधने ।
तृतीयं यज्ञदीक्षायां द्विजस्य श्रुतिचोदनात् ॥
तपोबीजप्रभावैस्तु ते गच्छंति युगे युगे ।
उत्कर्षं चापकर्षं च मनुष्येष्विह जन्मतः ।
तपः श्रुतं च योनिश्च द्विजत्वे कारणं स्मृतम् ॥
संकरे जातयस्त्वेताः पितृमातृप्रदर्शिताः ।
प्रच्छन्ना वा प्रकाशा वा वेदितव्याः स्वकर्मभिः ॥
शुचिरुत्कृष्टशुश्रूषुर्मृदुवागनहंकृतः ।
ब्राह्मणाद्याश्रयो नित्यमुत्कृष्टां जातिमश्नुते ॥ *Manu.*
शूद्रयोनौ हि जातस्य सद्गुणानुपतिष्ठतः ।
वैश्यत्वं लभ्यते ब्रह्मन् क्षत्रियत्वं तथैव च ।
आर्जवे वर्त्तमानस्य ब्राह्मण्यमभिजायते ॥

Mbh., Vana, ch. 216.

शृणु यक्ष कुलं नैव न स्वाध्यायो न च श्रुतम् ।
कारणत्वं द्विजत्वे च वृत्तमेव तु कारणम् ॥

Ibid, ch. 314.

जातिरत्र महासर्प मनुष्यत्वे महामते ।
संकरात् सर्ववर्णानां दुष्परीक्ष्येति मे मतिः ॥
इदमार्षं प्रमाणं च ये यजामह इत्यपि ।
तस्माच्छीलं प्रधानेष्टं विदुर्ये तत्त्वदर्शिनः ॥
तस्मिन्नेवं मतिद्वैधे मनुः स्वायंभुवोऽब्रवीत् ।
कृतकृत्याः सर्ववर्णा यदि वृत्तं न पश्यति ॥

Ibid, ch., 182.

न जात्या ब्राह्मणश्चात्र क्षत्रियो वैश्य एव वा ।
न शूद्रो न च वै म्लेच्छो भेदिता गुणकर्मभिः ॥
ब्रह्मणस्तु समुत्पन्नाः सर्वे ते किं न ब्राह्मणाः ।
न वर्णतो न जनकाद् ब्राह्मं तेजः प्रपद्यते ॥
ज्ञानकर्मोपासनाभिर्देवताराधने रतः ।
शान्तो दान्तो दयालुश्च ब्राह्मणस्तु गुणैः कृतः ॥
लोकसंरक्षणे दक्षः शूरो दान्त पराक्रमी ।
दुष्टनिग्रहशीलो यः स वै क्षत्रिय उच्यते ॥
क्रयविक्रयकुशला ये नित्यं पण्यजीविनः ।
पशुरक्षाः कृषिकरास्ते वैश्याः कीर्त्तिता भुवि ॥
द्विजसेवार्च्चनरताः शूरा शान्ता जितेंद्रियाः ।
सीरकाष्ठतृणवहास्ते नीचाः शूद्रसंज्ञकाः ॥
त्यक्तस्वधर्माचरणा निर्घृणाः परपीडकाः ।
चंडाश्च हिंसका नित्यं म्लेच्छास्ते ह्यविवेकिनः ॥

Shukra-nīti, I, 38-44.

ब्रह्म वीर्णमसंकीर्णं शाब्दं येन परं च तत् ।
सर्वत्र ब्रह्मदर्शी यः स ब्राह्मण इति स्मृतः ॥
दुर्बलानां क्षतात् त्राता क्षन्ता चोद्धतपापिनाम् ।
क्षन्ताऽत्मन्यपकाराणां स क्षत्रपदभाग् ध्रुवम् ॥
चतुर्वर्णचतुर्वर्गचतुराश्रमविष्टये ।
संविशन्ति विशो यस्मिन् स वैश्य इति वर्ण्यते ॥

शुचाऽल्पया द्रवेद्यस्तु सेवया द्रावयेच्च ताम् ।
पाल्यः पोष्यश्च शिष्यश्च स शूद्र इति कथ्यते ॥

The purport of the above is this. "In the early days of the human race there was no differentiation of castes and classes, or even of stages of life, for conditions of birth and death and living were very different. Looking at the source, there is no distinction between man and man ; for all are equally born from Brahman, and all are, therefore, by derivation, equally Brāhmaṇas ; but they have divided out into separate classes in accordance with their separate occupations. From another standpoint, it may be said that every child is born a Shūḍra by his first or physical birth ; and only by his second or spiritual birth into the Veḍa, the knowledge of scripture, and by initiation into his definite Self-conscious mission in life, does he become ḍvi-ja, re-generate. By the potency of the hereditary physical germ combined with the soul's inherent power of initiative and special effort, men may rise or fall in the scale of life, and change from one to another caste or class. Ṭapas or individual effort and special selection and spontaneous variation,

Shruṭam or the teaching received and associations and environment, and Yoni or heredity—these three in appropriate combination go to make up re-generacy. Even if a man be born in a Shūḍra family but practises the ways of the good, leads a pure life, learns from the virtuous and the noble, is gentle of speech and manner and free from arrogance, then he raises himself to the caste, Brāhmaṇa or Kshaṭṭriya or Vaishya, as the case may be, whose appropriate ways he takes as example. Not birth, not even learning, but *conduct* is the supreme test of re-generacy. We may infer parentage from character, not the other way. There has been so much mating and marrying, lawful and unlawful, of human beings, that the value of mere birth has become largely nullified ; character, conduct, is therefore the object of main regard to the wise. The First Manu himself has declared that if character and conduct are not to be considered then there is no point in making distinctions of varṇa at all.

"He who is devoted to knowledge, to science, to divine aspirations and meditations, who is peaceful, gentle, self-controlled and compassionate—he is a Brāhmaṇa. He who is able and eager to protect the weak from harm and to punish and restrain the wicked, who is brave and active and self-controlled—he is a Kshaṭṭriya. He who is skilled in matters of trade and cattle-keeping and agriculture and finance, and is self-controlled—he is a Vaishya. He who is fit for service of others, to guide the plough and carry wood and fodder—he is a Shūḍra. He who has abandoned his duties, is cruel and pitiless, and oppresses others, who is passionate and full of destructiveness—he is a Mlechchha.

"By etymology—he who has realised and acquired the Infinite 'Brahman', the One Life, as immanent in all life and all knowledge, and sees It everywhere—he is the true Brāhmaṇa. He who 'guards' the weak from 'harm', who 'harms' the wicked, and who 'forgives' harm to himself—he is the true Kshaṭṭriya. He to whom 'wealth' comes as to a trustee, in order that therewith all the four varṇas may be enabled easily to pass through the four āshramas and attain to the four vargas or ends of life—he is the true Vaishya. He who is easily 'disturbed' by even slight 'sorrow,' who helps to remove the sorrows of others by service, who should be cared for, fostered and taught and employed by the elders—he is the Shūḍra."

जन्म and कर्म, heredity and individual variation, जाति and वृत्त, birth and special disposition, तपःश्रुतं and योनिः, initiative will and environmental acquirements with racial aptitude, बीज and क्षेत्र, seed and soil, वर्ण and शील, color and character—are both important. But, obviously, the importance of birth depends on the importance of character, and not *vice versa*. Birth is the means, character the end. In the language of one school of modern evolutionists, what is hereditary in the existing individual must have been specially *developed and acquired* with effort by *some* ancestors. 'Good birth,' 'high birth,' is valued and lauded *because* it presumably implies good and high character. *Per contra*, where the character is bad, an evil heredity or ancestry is inferred, as is prominently recognised now in the cases of physical diseases and habits. Therefore, in the final resort, the total temperament and character of the person are the ultimate test of real 'caste' (*chasta*, pure), varṇa, '*color of mind*,' and not mere apparent physical birth only.

The mental 'color,' tone, tinge, quality, disposition, the special development of one of the three moods of consciousness, or otherwise, is to be emphatically considered.

सद्गुणो ब्राह्मणो वर्णः क्षत्रियस्तु रजोगुणः ।
तमोगुणस्तथा वैश्यः गुणसाम्यात्तु शूद्रता ॥

Bhavishya Purāṇa, Pt. III, iv, ch. 23.

The Brāhmaṇa has most सत्त्व, the principle of knowledge ; the Kṣhaṭṭriya, most रजस्, the principle of action ; the Vaishya, most तमस्, the principle of desire and devotion—even as Viṣhṇu, Brahmā and Shiva, respectively—without any 'odious comparisons' and notions of ingrained superiority or inferiority being implied; while an indecisiveness as between the three makes the Shūḍra.

That the physical color might also have a corresponding significance, possibly founded to some extent in the laws of psycho-physical parallelism, and that even a physical synthesis in the social organisation—not mutual exclusion—of all the ethnic types (as demarcated by the colors) might also have been meant by the elders who first organised the 'caste'-system, is indicated by the following :—

ब्राह्मणानां सितो वर्णः क्षत्रियाणां तु लोहितः ।
वैश्यानां पीतकश्चैव शूद्राणामसितस्तथा ॥

Padma Purāṇa, *Svarga Khanda*, *ch.* 27.
and *Mahābhāraṭa*, *Shānṭiparva*, *ch.* 186, v. 5.

But if birth is of no account, and character is all in all, then what becomes of the caste-system as a system? How would the professors of Varṇa Dharma be any better off than the peoples who have none such, who suffer from an unceasing ferment of blind unregulated competition, amongst whom every body struggles for every body else's place, and the years of preparation are spent in preparing for what is entirely uncertain in respect of the fitness of the preparer and the attainability of the goal; than the peoples who, to take a deceptive consolation to themselves for a sad failure, call that by the name of "individual freedom" which in reality is "social chaos"? The answer is that birth is *not* to be entirely neglected, any more than special aptitude.

Modern science in the west recognises evolution, in all departments of nature, by means of variation and differentiation and specialisation out of a central running line of heredity; and also utilises this great law in many ways for various practical purposes, as, *e.g.*, in raising special breeds of domestic animals for special purposes. In respect of human nature, however, somehow, it has so far omitted to recognise and utilise its operation. The polity of the Sanāṭana Ḍharma, on the contrary, bases itself expressly on the main lines of differentiation to be observed in the Human Race. It recognises, firstly, a twofold division therein, *viz.*, (I) the less evolved, technically called 'once-born,' in whom the power of introspection, self-consciousness, self-analysis, self-examination, deliberate self-control and self-guidance has not arisen, and (II) the more evolved, the 'twice-born,' the regenerate, in whom such power has developed more or less. Under the second class a further threefold sub-division is recognised, as mentioned before, *viz.*, (*a*) the men of thought, (*b*) the men of action, (*c*) the men of feeling (and art, industrial and fine), according to the predominance, in the individuals concerned, of the one or the other of the three well-known aspects or functions or faculties of the mind. All three are equally 're-generate.' In other modern counters of thought, the types may be designated as (*a*) intellectual, (*b*) militant, (*c*) industrial. The fourth class, the once-born, is that of the unskilled laborers. Of course there are endless grades and shades under each, with cross-mixtures and combinations besides; but these four are undoubtedly the main broad classes.

The Vaiḍika Ḍharma law and social organisation proceeded upon a clear and deliberate recognition of these types. It would be well if modern law and organisation also based themselves upon the same fundamental facts of human nature, duly taking account of the operation of the laws of *both* Heredity *and* Spontaneous Variation; avoiding, on the one hand, the manifest degenerations and ossifications which have come upon the old social structure in India with lapse of time, mainly because of the gradual forgetting of the second law, *viz.*, that of Spontaneous Variation ; and, on the other, correcting the defects, the seething chaos, of the modern condition which are due to the ignoring of the first law, *viz.*, that of heredity.

The discussions may be summed up thus :

उत्तमं जन्मकर्मभ्यां कर्मणैव तु मध्यमम् ।
अधमं केवलं जात्या वर्णवत्त्वं स्मृतं बुधैः ॥
आरोहणं तु सायासमनायासं तु पातनम् ।
सुकृतं दुष्करं प्रायो दुष्कृतं सुकरं पुनः ॥

"The highest degree of excellence and efficiency for the appropriate duties is secured where the qualifications of birth as well as of special aptitude and training are both present ; the next degree is where only the latter exist ; the poorest, where only the former is available. Ascent (from de-generacy to re-generacy) is difficult ; descent (from the latter to the former) is easy. Good deeds are difficult, ill deeds easy—mostly." It takes much and long labor to develop food grains and luscious fruits and garden flowers out of wild grasses and berries; it takes none for the cultivated lands to run back to waste and wild. Hence, rules in the Vaiḍika Ḍharma directed towards perfection of high breeding of the different types of men by care in dieting, in marriage, in manners and training. The acceptance of the principle of heredity gives an indispensable stability to the social organisation—without which it is an unorganised chaotic crowd of opportunists. The acceptance of the principle of spontaneous variation, to supplement and modify the other, gives the equally indispensable element of elasticity and periodic vital adjustments to the organisation—without which it becomes ossified and brittle or gouty and diseased and full of aches and pains all over, as it is at the present day in India.

Having stated the broad principles of Varṇa Ḍharma and Āshrama Ḍharma as above, we may now pass on to some of the details of our subject, in brief outline only, of course.

(*iii*) *The Three Kinds of Duties.*

It has been indicated before that the four ends of life, चतुर्वर्ग, ought to be *understood* by means of the Jñāna-Kānda, righteously *desired* and aspired after through the Bhakṭi-Kānda, and *realised* with the help of the Karma-Kānda. For a truth is living truth, *re*-al truth, *act*-ual truth, to a person, only when he is willing, nay, eager to *act* upon it, to apply it to the things (*res*), that concern him. Otherwise it is either a hypocritical lip-profession or idle dreaming. And, therefore, a consistent *practice* of life-activities, individual and communal, has been established by the seers of the Veḍas, the Manus and the Ṛṣhis, in accordance with their findings of āḍhy-āṭmika (subjective), āḍhi-bhauṭika (objective) and āḍhi-ḍaivika (dynamic) truths, *i.e.*, the facts and laws of Spirit, Matter and Energy, mind, body and force (which is always vital).

It has also been pointed out that the varṇa-and-āshrama scheme is the soundest, the most scientific and practical, the least utopian system of social organisation that has been devised, within historic memory, for the realisation by each member of the community, as fully as in him lies, of the four chief purposes of life, *viz.*, I (*i*) Kāma refined and purified by (*ii*) Arṭha and regulated by (*iii*) Dharma, and II (*iv*) Mokṣha. In other words, I, the Joys of finite physical existence, of dwelling within a body possessed of sensor and motor organs, देहितानुभव, ennobled, enriched and guarded from error respectively by (*a*) Art, (*b*) Science, and (*c*) Law, and II, the final Deliverance of the Soul from earthly bonds of doubts and desires, and the attainment of the Bliss of Infinite Being, by means of (*d*) the Divine Philosophy and Spiritual Wisdom which realises the Unity of all Life and all lives.

Finally, it has been suggested that the scheme is thus rational and workable, because it is based on the sure and permanent facts and laws of psycho-physics, and not on any mere imaginative political, mechanical, or industrial artifices and *tours de force*; and because, in the framing of the scheme, all the three main great lines of human functioning (with their endless sub-divisions) and their summation, *viz.*, the I (*a*) Art, (*b*) Science, and (*c*) Law of the Finite, and II (*d*) the Metaphysic of the Infinite, are directly oriented and applied to the corresponding main ends of life (with their sub-divisions). From this standpoint, the most important Classification of the Sciences and of all human knowledge is that which practicalises them into (*a*) Kāma-Shāsṭra, (*b*) Arṭha-Shāsṭra, (*c*) Ḍharma-Shāsṭra, and (*d*) Mokṣha-Shāsṭra. The other well-known classification is into (*i*) Aparā-viḍyā and (*ii*) Parā-viḍyā, in the words of the Mundaka Upaṇiṣhaṭ, with details in terms of the Veḍas, Veḍāngas, Veḍopāngas, etc. But of this also, the first includes the three (*a*, *b*, and *c*), and the fourth is the same as (*d*). It should be noted here that Kāma-Shāsṭra does *not* mean what it has degenerated into, *viz.*, the art of mere obscenity and lust, but the Science of Conjugal Love and Domestic Happiness, physical and psychical, (रति and प्रीति, the two wives of Kāma-ḍeva) and also all the "sixty-four fine arts," the चतुःषष्टिकला, that enrich and enhance the joys of family life. So Arṭha-Shāsṭra is not merely the Science of Wealth and all its means, is not merely economics or politics, but science in general *applied* to the service of life. And Ḍharma-Shāsṭra is not only the Science of human

Law, jurisprudence, but of superphysical law as well, acting as the regulator of and the nexus between the rights and duties of jīvas on the physical as well as the subtler planes which are all inseparably related together. Mokṣha-Shāsṭra is the summation of them all ; not mere abstract psychology and ontology and logomachy or even mere political 'freedom,' but the Science of Spiritual Freedom, the Science of universal life and of deep Peace of soul ; which enables the jīva to become a 'law unto itself,' not in the sense that it is 'free' to act capriciously and that whatever it does is right, but that it has attained to the fount of Righteousness, the sense of the Unity of all Life, and therefore does only what is right, and avoids what is wrong, its *nature* now according with the 'categorical imperative.'

निस्त्रैगुण्ये पथि विचरतो
को विधिः को निषेधः ॥
यद्यदाचरति श्रेष्ठस्तत्तदेवेतरो जनः ।
स यत्प्रमाणं कुरुते लोकस्तदनुवर्त्तते ॥ *Gīṭā.*

Imitating the medieval schoolmen, we might call these four studies, the 'humanities,' the 'realities,' the 'legalities' and the 'divinities.'

The difference between this scientific arrangement and conduction of life and the violent artifices of utopians is alluded to in *Manu* :

या वेदबाह्याः स्मृतयो याश्च काश्च कुदृष्टयः ।
सर्वास्ता निष्फलाः प्रेत्य तमोनिष्ठा हि ताः स्मृताः ॥
उत्पद्यंते च्यवंते च यान्यतोऽन्यानि कानिचित् ।
तान्यर्वाक्कालिकतया निष्फलान्यनृतानि च ॥

The Mahābhāraṭa says :—

धर्मे चार्थे च कामे च मोक्षे च भरतर्षभ ।
यदिहास्ति तदन्यत्र यन्नेहास्ति न तत्क्वचित् ॥

"The views and ways that are not in accord with the Veḍa-wisdom— they only lead to barrenness and sorrow here and hereafter—for they are founded on the misleading darkness of selfish desires. They spring up and die down like mushrooms—because they place their trust and fix their eyes on the fleeting things of the moment, and take their rise from *temporary* aims and objects that are not true and righteous, and rest not on the rock of the *Eternal* Ideal. Only in the Veḍa-outlook upon life is the promise of the fulfilment of Virtue, thence Profit, thence Pleasure, as well as of Bliss Immortal."

Of course, in order that the noble tree of this perfectly-planned organism of society should bear and yield its legitimate fruit of joyous sweetness, it is necessary that it be watered with the waters of living intelligence, of that alert reason which has been defined as the faculty of devising and fitting means to ends, and be tended ever in the loving, all-embracing spirit of accommodativeness and adaptive elasticity ; it must not be heaped around with the dry sands of dead formalism gathered by rigid obstinacy born of selfish antipathies and arrogance and hatred.

Now, the subject-matter of this Karma-Kānda might be expounded from any one of the three standpoints mentioned in the previous chapter. To set it forth at length in terms of varṇa and āshrama would no doubt be the most exhaustive. It would require, however, a complete description of the duties of all the four chief classes of men in all the four principal orders of life, *i.e.*, of each of the four types of individuals and corresponding vocations during each stage of life, so far as appurtenant. This is scarcely the place for such details. (They have been attempted elsewhere, *vide The Science of Social Organisation.*) With reference to another standpoint, the duties, respectively, of (*a*) the pursuant and (*b*) the renunciant halves of life, are divided between the first two āshramas on the one hand, and the last two on the other. Therefore, the subject need not be specifically treated here from that point of view either. For the present purpose, *viz.*, the presentation of broad outlines with indication of underlying principles, the second sub-division referred to in the preceding chapter will probably be the most convenient, *viz.*, the classification of 'actions,' with reference to their comparative importance, into (*a*) the daily and 'permanently' binding or imperative duties, (*b*) the 'occasional' functions, and (*c*) the 'optional' acts.

This method will also probably make the establishment of correspondences and contacts with other systems of religion easier. For even amidst the endlessly varying details of rituals and polities of the various religions, we may still discern certain general principles as common to all the schemes.

(*a*) Thus every religion, to a greater or lesser extent, lays down some directions in the nature of rules of daily individual conduct and of forms of domestic and social polity, enjoining certain practices upon, and assigning various rights and duties, functions and vocations, to different men and groups of men, of different temperaments and capacities, and in different situations in life—all such conduct and custom being regarded as *necessary* for the maintenance of individual and communal health, of private and public well-being.

(*b*) Almost all religions also prescribe a set of sacraments and initiations, some fewer, some more numerous, which may be classified, broadly, into (*i*) ante-natal, (*ii*) intra-vital, and (*iii*) post-mortem—connected with the three main 'adventures' of life, *viz.*, birth, marriage, death.

The sub-conscious or recognised purpose of all these is, by various processes, tests and trials, disciplinings and examinations, carried out from time to time, on special and appropriate occasions, to facilitate the experience and glorify the results of these 'adventures,' and to purify and consecrate, train and stimulate, educate and develop, under greater or lesser stress and strain, in an atmosphere of special emotional intensity and excellence, the grosser and subtler bodies inhabited by the soul, in such a manner as to make them strong and fit for the discharge of the daily duties, and also, generally, to make life, in and through them, here and hereafter, higher, richer and nobler, and enable the soul to attain to ever greater and greater perfection of manifestation and fuller and fuller communion with Nature and with Nature's God, *i.e.*, that soul Itself in Fundamental Essence. "The body is the soul made visible." "Nature is the garment of God." The manifestation of Spirit is in and by Matter. The finer the material of the denser and the subtler sheaths, the finer the manifestation.

(*c*) Finally, every religion also recommends or simply mentions other rites and ceremonies and deeds of merit, whereby greater access to and intercourse with the denizens of other and invisible worlds may be secured, and latent superphysical faculties unfolded for various 'desirable' (as distinguished from 'imperative') purposes of the earthly or the heavenly life.

All this department of 'actional' ḍharma is, obviously, in respect of the 'forms,' largely relative to time, place and circumstance, as explained before in connection with the *summum bonum* and the 'sanction' of morality. In the scheme of Sanāṭana Vaiḍika Ḍharma, however, as under the two other main titles of Jñāna and Bhakṭi, so here, the exposition of the facts and laws seems perhaps to be fuller and more systematic than elsewhere.

Class (*a*) above corresponds, generally, with the Niṭya-karma; (*b*) with the Naimiṭṭika; and (*c*) with Kāmya. They may be called the perpetual or imperative, the occasional and the optional duties, in modern terms. They repeat, under the general head of Karma-kānda, the fundamental triad of cognition, action and desire, which appears in Dharma, Artha and Kāma, respectively.

तमसो लक्षणं कामो रजसस्त्वर्थ उच्यते ।
सत्त्वस्य लक्षणं धर्मो श्रैष्ठ्यमेषां यथोत्तरम् ॥

Manu.

(*iv*) *Nitya-Karma.*

The 'imperative daily duties' have been defined thus :—

यदकरणे प्रत्यवायः यच्चाहरहःपुरस्कारविहितं तन्नित्यकर्म ।

"The action which is 'perpetually or permanently due' to be done is that which is ordained for daily performance and the omission of which entails sin." For current purposes the Smṛtis enumerate these perpetual duties under four main heads, (*a*) Shaucham, (*b*) Āchārah, (*c*) Pañcha-mahā-yajñah, and (*d*) Sandhyā-vandanam—cleanliness, good conduct, the five great sacrifices and the orisons. Thus Manu :

उपनीय गुरुः शिष्यं शिक्षयेच्छौचमादितः ।
आचारमग्निकार्यं च संध्योपासनमेव च ॥

In modern language we should say the ever-present duties are, (*a*) the observance of the laws of hygiene and sanitation, (*b*) the fulfilment of the requirements of good manners and morals, polite ways, gentle speech and courteous demeanour towards elders, youngers and equals, (*c*) the performance of some acts of service to fellow-creatures of the human, sub-human and superhuman kingdoms, and (*d*) the offering of prayer and worship to the Infinite (or some lesser) source of psychical as well as physical vitality, purity and power, in order to derive nourishment and sustenance therefrom.

It is possible to allocate these four under our familiar triad. In terms of the Yoga-sūṭra, their details, re-arranged, would fall under (*a*) तपः, (*b*) स्वाध्यायः, (*c*) ईश्वरप्रणिधानम्, or self-denial, study, and unceasing submission, surrender and direction of the mind to God, 'dwelling in God,' निवसिष्यासि मय्येव (*Gīṭā*). They may be said also to correspond to the (*a*) दानम्, (*b*) अध्ययनम्, (*c*) इज्या, charity, study and sacrifice—which are incumbent on all 'regenerate' persons alike. Self-denials and austerities, charity, purity and good conduct may be said to be the more express and outward or 'active' niṭya-karma; study and teaching of the brāhma 'great sacrifice,' the more intellectual or 'cognitional' duty; the constant 'dwelling in God' and prayer and worship, the more 'desiderative' or emotional duty. Finally, we may note that they respectively correspond to Arṭha, Ḍharma, and Kāma; and that when the worship is directed, in the later stages of life, to the Infinite Self, and not to any lesser concrete and personal deity, when it takes on the nature of Self-realisation, when God begins to be seen as identical with the Āṭmā in whom all living beings necessarily live and move and have their being, the ocean of Universal Consciousness which is patently the only 'dwelling-place,' evidence, support and source of all forms, all 'objects;' and when that worship is accompanied with appropriate study of the Mokṣha-shāsṭra and the nish-kāma or unselfish and self-sacrificing performance of the appropriate portions of niṭya-karma, then that niṭya-karma as a whole becomes naiṣh-karmya or altruistic universalism, and subserves and corresponds to Mokṣha, the fourth and final goal of life.

प्रवृत्तं कर्म संसेव्य देवानामेति साम्यताम् ।
निवृत्तं सेवमानस्तु भूतान्यत्येति पंच वै ॥

Manu.

(*a*) *Shaucham.*

Under the head of Shaucham, the Smṛṭis lay down rules as to waking and sleeping, personal cleanliness, teeth-cleaning, ablutions, sex-purity, appropriate diet and dress, *etc.*, for the different classes and orders—all which matters, 'scientifically' or 'legally' (as it would be now called, ḍharmeṇa, as it was formerly) regulated, are all equally necessary to a life of psychical and physical health—health which means wholeness, holiness, perfectness in mind and body, the two going together inseparably. That 'cleanliness is next to godliness,' or indeed 'is on both sides of it,' is nowhere more patent than in the scheme of Sanāṭana Vaiḍika Ḍharma. Indeed, in its degenerate exaggerations and perversions, current Hinḍuism, to the casual observer, is in major part made up of customs as to 'touch-me-not' of the most senselessly formalist and even positively harmful sort ; so that it happens repeatedly that food is taken from the hands of one who may be suffering from a contagious and dangerous disease simply because he is a 'caste'-man, but not from the hands of a non-caste-man, though he may be thoroughly clean and healthy, and though the Smṛṭis permit it expressly. The fault is not in the rules; it is in the interpreters. That great errors and excesses are liable to arise even under the guidance of 'official modern science' when pushed to extremes, and not only of Ḍharma, is easy to understand on remembering how exaggerated segregations and quarantines were commenced under the new-born terrors of the first discoveries of the bacilli of infectious diseases, and how a healthier sense of proportion was only gradually restored when further discoveries were made of healthful microbes and phagocytes and natural physiological anti-toxins and the resisting powers of prāṇa, *vis viva*, and the germicide properties of clean air, clean light, clean drink and clean food.

Incidentally, to understand why such items

as दन्तधावनम्, 'teeth-cleaning,' are mentioned specifically in the rules of Shaucham in the old 'law'-books, we should look at the efforts, being now made by the wiser among the 'medicine-men' of the West, at this day of advanced civilisation there, and being made with but slow and scant success, to get their peoples to realise that unclean teeth mean decayed teeth, whence foul mouths and fœtid breath and breeding-grounds for disease-microbes, then indigestion and ill-digestion and the formation of poisons in the stomach and the tissues, and then, finally, fifty per cent. or more of all the ills that human flesh is heir to. The āḍhy-āṭmika and āḍhi-ḍaivika psycho-biological errors in diet and in sex-matters, as medical men know well, account for ninety-five per cent. of the diseases and misfortunes of humanity, only about five per cent. or less being due to āḍhi-bhauṭika or external accidents.

प्रमादादन्नदोषाच्च मृत्युर्विप्रान् जिघांसति ॥ *Manu.*

'Teeth cleaning'' in the ancient 'law'-books may look 'funny' to the hasty mind, but is really more in place and more useful than prohibitions against spitting on the public streets and a hundred other similar provisions against nuisances and dangers to health are in modern law-books. If the nityakarma, the regular observance of certain simple laws of personal hygiene, dietary, dress and sex-conduct, were enforced by 'modern' law, as they were attempted to be by the 'ancient,' *and* the economic and social conditions created and maintained which would make their observance possible, then very likely many other laws would become superfluous and disappear of themselves which now encumber statute-books and which hamper and hinder daily life instead of helping it.

It is true, modern jurisprudents endeavor to distinguish sharply between law and morals and endeavor to demarcate their respective provinces off from each other, but their success is more than doubtful. In the older scheme, 'legal pressure' was only a more specific form of 'socio-religious pressure'; the two merged insensibly into each other; hard and fast distinctions were not believed in; and inducements to positive deeds of merit went hand in hand with deterrents against vice and sin and crime. And in *practice*, this is often true of modern civilisation too; only the ways of looking and speaking are different; the 'modern' mind revels in distinctions, looks more at the surface-causes and external results, and less at the deep-lying psychical causes and internal functionings, and emphasises what the 'ancient' mind did not lay stress upon, and *vice versa*. Yet more, many thoughtful people in the West also have begun to feel acutely that the glorification of lawyer's and legislator's 'law' is being overdone there. And it is indeed a fact that modern civilisation has become more 'law'-ridden than, even in its latter-day degeneration, the ancient civilisation of India has been pseudo-ḍharma-ridden; that at least as many excesses and evils are perpetrated under the ægis of the noble names of Law, Science and Art (from which, as deliberately divorced from the 'superstitions' of Religion and 'false' superphysics and 'empty' metaphysics, the newer much-vaunted culture somehow derives itself), as ever were in the shade of the nobler names of Ḍharma, Arṭha and Kāma or Kalā (to which Law, Science and Art are respectively as means, and from which, as closely subordinated to and guided and governed by the Ideal of Mokṣha and Spiritual Wisdom, the older Ethos purposefully evolved itself); and that a thorough overhauling, purgation, and reformation of the whole system of society from top to bottom has become necessary.

The principles of the Sanāṭana Vaiḍika Ḍharma are the only natural, true and strong foundations on which the crumbling edifice can be reconstructed safely.

स ब्रह्मविद्यां सर्वविद्याप्रतिष्ठामथर्वाय ज्येष्ठपुत्राय प्राह ।
Mundaka.

Under these principles, for the true education of the individual and the building up in him of that firm and noble *character* which is the only sure foundation of all prosperity and happiness, individual and communal, instruction in Shaucham stands in the forefront.

The practice of the rules of purity, begun in the days of childhood and studentship, becomes perfected in the days of sannyāsa and old age, so that there result from it what the Yoga-Sūṭras describe thus :—

शौचात्स्वांगजुगुप्सा परैरसंसर्गः ।
सत्त्वशुद्धिसौमनस्यैकाग्र्येंद्रियजयात्मदर्शन-
योग्यत्वादीनि ।

"Recognition of the inherent impurity of the physical body, avoidance of unclean contacts, lucid clarity of intelligence, chaste serenity of mind, control of attention and absence of mind-wandering and fickleness, mastery of the senses, and worthiness and readiness to recognise the Great Self."

The danger, of course, is that, if the practice is misplaced, mistimed and misconducted, instead of the great results above-mentioned and the vision of the Larger Self, there will be produced only an accentuation of the smaller self, with all its corollaries of complacent self-righteousness, narrow self-conceit and sense of sole and exclusive proprietorship of heaven.

The Roman Catholic scheme recognises the 'odour of sanctity' which, not only metaphysically but also literally, develops in the persons of the pure beyond common. The chastening attractiveness of the pure, the noble, the holy, is due to the refined magnetism and vital prāṇas and ethereal taṭṭvas which develop and play in their persons and resistlessly compel Magdalenes to cast away their loads of sins and luxuries to follow the feet of the Christs, or give new lease of life to conscience-stricken and petrified Ahalyās at the touch of the feet of Rāmas. Such are the results of Shaucham in perfection.

(*b*) *Āchāra.*

The rules of Āchāra deal with the methods of salutation and address, postures, gestures and manners for all occasions, distinguishing vocational marks in apparel, work and play, fasts and festivals, vows and vigils, recreations and relaxations, laborious days and holidays—no more surprising than the modern very elaborate codes of table-manners and tea-ceremonies, warrants of precedence for Court-functions and levees, or the 'laws' against travelling in the wrong class of carriage on railways and tramways or those regulating Bank-holidays. No more surprising than these, and perhaps more healthful and spontaneous in feeling and less irksomely compulsive from without, because developed in an atmosphere of *aḍhyāṭma* and spirituality and ever-present communion with the higher worlds.

The rules of āchāra are included in the ḍharma-law somewhat on the same principles on which, *e.g.*, vaccination and inoculation and the heights of buildings in municipal towns are dealt with by modern law, and, it may perhaps be said, for sounder and less disputable reasons. One of the recognised classics of Samskṛṭ medicine is known as the Charaka-Samhiṭā, though it was originally composed by Agnivesha and only revised, re-edited, brought up to date and republished by Charaka : अग्निवेशकृते तन्त्रे चरकप्रतिसंस्कृते. In this work there is a long chapter devoted to सदाचार, "The ways of the good and the wise." The most important items out of these have been taken over by the *Smṛṭis* too. 'Good manners and morals' are emphasised greatly in these.

आचारः परमो धर्मः श्रुत्युक्तः स्मार्त एव च ।
तस्मादस्मिन् सदा युक्तो नित्यं स्यादात्मवान् द्विजः ॥
एवमाचारतो दृष्ट्वा धर्मस्य मुनयो गतिम् ।
सर्वस्य तपसो मूलमाचारं जगृहुः परम ॥ *Manu.*
आचारहीनं न पुनंति वेदा
यद्यप्यधीताः सह षड्भिरंगैः ।
छंदांस्येनं मृत्युकाले त्यजंति
नीडं शकुंता इव जातपक्षाः ॥ *Vasishtha Smṛṭi.*

Civilities make civilisation, the recognition and performance not only of civil duties in the narrower sense, but of the duties of appropriate gentleness and courtesy and recognition of other's rights in the widest sense. And the character, culture, social convention, civilisation (*civis*, सभा) सभ्यता, शील, समयाचार, is strongly based only when it rests on the sure foundations of the recognition of Spirit and the knowledge of Its ways of manifestation in the world-process; when the āchāra issues from within spontaneously, and is not imposed from without by fear, when it is oriented to a definite goal and not left to shape itself haphazard. The 'gentlemen' and 'gentlewomen' are they who behave 'gently' to others *because* they recognise that the 'others' are the same in essence as themselves; because they have received the 'second birth' into the Consciousness of the Larger Self, because they are द्विज and आत्मवान्. And in gentle behaviour, gentle speech is first. The first manifestation of the soul's unmanifest movement is in sound, in this world of ours. And the first and as yet also the richest and the most intelligent and intelligible communion of the soul with its sister-souls is by the voice. Not to know each other's language is to be strangers. To understand is to sympathise. Not to understand is to misunderstand. There is no greater source of a common understanding and a common interest, a common national, political and social life, than a common tongue. Hence the great stress laid by the law-giver on the appropriate use of the Āryan Samskṛt language.

तृणानि भूमिरुदकं वाक् चतुर्थी च सूनृता ।
एतान्यपि सतां गेहे नोच्छिद्यंते कदाचन ॥
वाच्यर्थाः निहिताः सर्वे वाङ्मूला वाग्विनिस्सृताः ।

तस्माद् यः स्तेनयेद् वाचं स सर्वस्तेयकृन्नरः ॥ *Manu.*

तां चाप्येतां मातरं मंगलानां ।
धेनुं धीराः सूनृतां वाचमाहुः ॥
ऋषयो राक्षसीमाहुर्वाचमुन्मत्तदृप्तयोः ।
सा योनिः सर्ववैराणां सा हि लोकस्य निर्ऋतिः ॥

Bhavabhuti.

"Straw mats, a place to sit, water and gentle speech—these at least are never lacking in the good man's home. All thoughts are enshrined in and inseparably connected with language. He who misuses language, misuses everything. Gentle speech is the mother of all auspiciousness as the proud and arrogant speech is the mother of discord and death."

The simpler āchāra of the early stages becomes, in the later ones, gradually more and more perfected, till we have the yamas and niyamas, vows and vigils, abstinences and austerities, of yoga, which lead the soul from mere goodness as student and citizen into the saintliness of the vanasṭha and the sannyāsi, the status of the ṛṣhi, the muni, the truest and highest (as greatly distinguished from the nominal) brāhmaṇa.

To bring out the full significance of आचार, सदाचार, शिष्टाचार, and of आचारवान्, we may compare, as below, the somewhat abstract definition of 'a true gentleman' by a famous writer of the more concrete-minded West, and the somewhat concrete description of 'the perfect man' by the आदिकवि, the first poet, of the more abstract-minded East.

"The true gentleman carefully avoids whatever may cause a jar or a jolt in the minds of those with whom he is cast—all clashing of opinion, or collision of feeling, all restraint, or suspicion, or gloom, or resentment; his great concern being to make every one at their ease and at home. He has his eyes on all his company; he is tender towards the bashful, gentle towards the distant, and merciful towards the absurd; he can recollect to whom he is speaking; he guards against unseasonable allusions, or topics which may irritate: he is seldom prominent in conversation, and never wearisome. He makes light of favours while he does them, and seems to be receiving when he is conferring." Thus Cardinal Newman.

Now Vālmīki (I. i and II. i, ii):

"Rāma, the eldest son of Dasharatha and Kausalyā, was very beautiful to see, and full of virile energy and the bloom of youth. Uncavilling and uncarping, and ever magnanimous and placid of soul, he always commenced a conversation with a soft word and a sweet smile. If harshly addressed he would be at a loss for all reply except a gentle one. Much would he belaud and make of even a very small service done to him ; but a hundred serious disservices and wrongs to himself he would fail to remember, because of his आत्मवत्ता, because he was so full of the sense of the Universal Self, the Common Life, (and so was as ready to excuse others as ordinary folk are to excuse themselves—for "to know all is to forgive all"). Those who were great in virtuous character, high in wisdom, senior in years, with such he would associate and converse diligently during the hours of leisure from martial exercises and the practice of arms. Full of strong reason and of sweet reasonableness also was he, gentle of speech, ever ready to begin a conversation (to put his guest or visitor at ease), and ever using words of sympathy and affection.

"He always avoided talk and act that were false or fanciful or quarrelsome or unrighteous, and diligently cultivated learning and honoured the learned and the aged. Deeply instructed was he in all duty and ḍharma, ever clean of body and pure of mind, ever mindful of the high dynastic traditions of kingly duty and kshaṭṭriya responsibility, and firm in the conviction that righteous fame on earth meant divine joy in heaven.

"Observant of all due proprieties and social conventions, grave and unexcitable of expression, silent and reserved when necessary, possessed of that magnetic charm which inspired in others the deepest devotion to his own person and himself, most firm and loyal of friendship, neither his pleasure nor his displeasure was barren of appropriate result to the object thereof. He knew what to give and what to withhold, when to encourage and when to repress, whom to reward and whom to punish. Yet even when punishing the criminal unflinchingly, he never was angry with them, but always sorry. Possessed like to the Master of Speech, Bṛhaspaṭi, himself, of the power of debate and reasoned reply in linked argument, steady in well-considered opinions formed after consultation and discussion (विमर्द), not readily shaken nor yet obstinately committed to a wrong view but always open-minded, never harsh of speech or indolent of mind or body, he was as clearly aware of his own as of others' faults and weaknesses.

"Mindful was he of all righteous sources of income, and of the just and permissible occasions and extent of expenditure on pious and public works, and for righteous fame, for investment bringing further increase of revenue, and for the enjoyments of self and kinsfolk; and always did he confine 'pleasure' (काम) within the limits set by law (धर्म) and finance (अर्थ).

"He knew the essential secrets of all the arts of peace and of war, and was versed in all physical accomplishments, and especially in the control of elephants and horses. A great leader and warrior was he, most skilled in the generalship of armies, not to be daunted in the forefront of battle by the rage and wrath of even the gods and the titans; yet would he never slight the meanest enemy nor ever yield to ungoverned moods and surges of emotion within himself.

"Youthful and beautiful, healthy and strong, large of limb, eloquent of speech, well-balanced of mind, delicately responsive to the occasions of time and place, high-born, heroic, truth-spoken, simple-hearted, straightforward, full of power and prowess yet most modest, master over all passions, instructed in all art and science, cognisant of all the main purposes and goals of life, unfailing of memory, rich and rapid of intelligence, true of promise, conciliatory of language, controlled of sense, forgiving of temper, gentle yet firm, high of purpose, undepressible of soul, ever victorious in battle, reverent to elders, affectionate to friends, most tender and considerate to the weak and the young, sympathetic with all in joy and in sorrow, like to Mother Earth in patient endurance and compassionate forgivingness, like to Bṛhaspaṭi in wisdom and to Indra in might—verily Rāma was as the Lokapālas themselves, the divine sovereigns of the higher worlds. Divining intuitively the essential character of each man and the differences of quality between different men, and knowing unmistakenly the appropriate place of every one in the gradation of soul-development, he himself was formed by the Creator out of the very quintessence of perfect manhood. Ever he strove for the increase, the progress, the prosperity of the people, and took joy in them as they took joy in him ; for indeed the people loved him with a love unbounded, and the Earth longed for him."

Such was Vālmīki's सत्पुरुष, ,the true man,' 'the good man,' महापुरुष, 'the great man,' मर्यादापुरुष, 'the standard man', प्रमाणपुरुष, 'the test man', 'the measure man', आदर्शपुरुष, 'the model man,' 'the ideal man,' पुरुषोत्तम, 'the perfect man'—all because he was आत्मवान्, 'possessed of the Universal Self'—that is the key-word.

But what about 'the perfect woman'? The 'true gentlewoman' of the 'old-fashioned' thinkers like Vālmīki, is described in one word, पतिव्रता, तुल्यशीला, "having the same vows as the husband, devoted to the husband," "of equal nature with him, sympathetic, not contrary." When Rāma was setting out on his exile, "Sīṭā *would* go with him and *would* put on forest-wanderers' dress as he did, for she was (*mutatis mutandis*) of 'like nature' and 'like ways' with and 'entirely devoted to her husband,' even as, because of that same fact, she could, if need be, carry on the government of a kingdom ; but would not, at that time,

तासामेवंविधा वाचः शृण्वन् दशरथात्मजः ।
बबंधैव तदा चीरं सीतया तुल्यशीलया ॥

even though Vasishtha says that "she should stay behind and sit on the throne of Rama while he was away, and should carry on the work of the state, for she is the soul of Rāma" :

अनुष्ठास्यति रामस्य सीता प्रकृतमासनम् ।
आत्मेयमिति रामस्य पालयिष्यति मेदिनीम् ॥

Perhaps Shakespeare also meant some similar thing when he made one of his famous *paṭi-vraṭā* heroines say :—

"My heart's subdued
Even to the very quality of my lord."

To love an ideal is to strive to become like that ideal, indeed it is, gradually, to become that ideal, for we become one with, we become, that which we love. And by diligent observance of **शिष्टाचार**, men become **शिष्ट**, the Elect.

ॐ

नम आत्मप्रदीपाय साक्षिणे परमात्मने ।
पुरुषायात्ममूलाय मूलप्रकृतये नमः ॥
त्वमेव सर्वभूतानां हृदयव्योम्नि तिष्ठसि ।
भ्रामयन् सर्वभूतानि यंत्रारूढानि मायया ॥
ज्ञानिनामपि चेतांसि देवी भगवती हि सा ।
बलादाकृष्य मोहाय महामाया प्रयच्छति ॥
दैवी ह्येषा गुणमयी तव माया दुरत्यया ।
त्वामेव ये प्रपद्यंते मायामेतां तरंति ते ॥
अपि चेत्सुदुराचारो भजते त्वामनन्यभाक् ।
तं नूनं सर्वपापेभ्यो मोक्षयिष्यसि मा चिरं ॥
यस्मिन्निदं यतश्चेदं येनेदं य इदं स्वयं ।
योऽस्मात्परस्माच्च परस्तं प्रपद्ये स्वयंभुवं ॥

यो वै न देवासुरमर्त्यतिर्यङ्
न स्त्री न षंढो न पुमान्न जंतुः ।
नायं गुणः कर्म न सन्न चासन्
निषेधशेषो जयतादशेषः ॥

मादृक्प्रपन्नपशुपाशविमोक्षणाय
मुक्ताय भूरिकरुणाय नमोऽलयाय ।
स्वांशेन सर्वतनुभृन्मनसि प्रतीत-
प्रत्यग्दृशे भगवते बृहते नमस्ते ॥

ॐ

ADDENDA ET CORRIGENDA.

P. l.

1. 6. After 'heart' read 'and limbs'.

2. 2. For 'on' read 'of'.

14. 5. Put a comma after 'versatile.'

26. 19. Put a hyphen between 'and' and 'Duty.

32. 13. After line 13 add,

महासरस्वति चित्ते महालक्ष्मि सदात्मिके ।
महाकाल्यानंदरूपे त्वत्तत्त्वज्ञानसिद्धये ।
अनुसंदध्महे चंडि वयं त्वां हृदयांबुजे ॥

23. 13. For 'or' read 'of.'

24. 4. After '*Vedānṭā*' add).

39. 6. After "Karma-marga," add :—

योगास्त्रयो मया प्रोक्ता नृणां श्रेयोविधित्सया ।
ज्ञानं कर्म च भक्तिश्च नोपायोऽन्योऽस्ति कुत्रचित्
निर्विण्णानां ज्ञानयोगो न्यासिनामिह कर्मसु ।
तेष्वनिर्विण्णचित्तानां कर्मयोगस्तु कामिनाम् ॥
यदृच्छया मत्कथादौ जातश्रद्धस्तु यः पुमान्
न निर्विण्णो नातिसक्तो भक्तियोगोऽस्य सिद्धिदः

Bhāgavata, XI. ch: 20, v. 6-8.

55. 2. for ज्ञा read ज्ञ.

57. 14. After 'words' add 'in the Great Story.

64.	18.	For 'Supra' read 'Supra-conscious'.
66.	10.	After ' of ' add ' generality,'
77.	11.	Add ' *Gītā* ' at end.
80.	13.	After ' to ' add ' do.'
80.	17.	After ' and ' add ' the ' ; and for ' religion ' read ' religious '.
89.	16.	After ' स्मृतः ॥ ' add '*Bhāgavata.*'.
94.	8.	After अत्यंताभीष्टं add परमार्थः, लक्ष्यतमं.
102.	3.	After 'perfectionists' add 'eudœmonists
115.	1.	Add ' *Manu* ' at end.
126.	1.	After line 1, add ;

वृद्धानामाज्ञया यश्चाप्याशु द्रवति किंकरः ।

134.	6.	For ' condition ' read ' conditions '.
140.	18.	After ' trust ' add ' in '.
152.	17.	Omit ' endeavour '.
158.	11.	For ' civil ' read ' civic '.
160.	7.	After ' sit ' add ' in '.